GROWING UP
IN TRUST

First published by O-Books, 2008
Reprinted, 2011
O-Books is an imprint of John Hunt Publishing Ltd., Laurel House, Station Approach,
Alresford, Hants, SO24 9JH, UK
office1@o-books.net
www.o-books.com

For distributor details and how to order please visit the 'Ordering' section on our website.

Text copyright: Justine Mol 2008
Translation by Dawn Mastin

ISBN: 978 1 84694 105 4

A CIP catalogue record for this book is available from the British Library.

Design: Stuart Davies

Printed in the UK by CPI Antony Rowe
Printed in the USA by Offset Paperback Mfrs, Inc

We operate a distinctive and ethical publishing philosophy in all
areas of our business, from our global network of authors to
production and worldwide distribution.

GROWING UP
IN TRUST

Justine Mol

BOOKS

Winchester, UK
Washington, USA

What a wonderful book. Such a simple message, and yet so important – and so challenging! This is the best of the many books I have read on how to bring up children with integrity. This is how I want my grandchildren to be brought up. And this is how I want to behave in many of my other relationships too. All parents should read it.
Susan Norman, Former Director of SEAL (Society for Effective Affective Learning)

This book is a great support for anyone with childen. Warm and encouraging, it is full of practical ideas on how to implement wisdom in real life situations. It clearly shows that children have a willingness to trust, to learn and contribute, and it's a view of human nature worth investing in.
Liv Larsson, author, Leadership coach, NVC trainer and publisher

Justine Mol's book, "Growing up in Trust", might well bear the subtitle, "Bringing Up Children to Thrive on Diversity and Become Passionate, Benevolent Lovers of Life". From twelve perspectives, she builds a strong case for a strictly non-authoritarian approach to bringing up children and demonstrates it to her readers by encouraging them not to accept her authority, but to apply her theories to their own life's experience. The simple, direct style of her original Dutch text is well captured in this excellent English translation by Dawn Mastin. "Growing up in Trust" is an invaluable tool for all educators, parents and indeed anyone who wishes to help prepare others to contribute maximally to a well-functioning, global world.
Lisinka Ulatowska, MA German Literature, PhD Psychology, United Nations NGO Representative, Association of World Citizens

CONTENTS

INTRODUCTION

Our heads are round so our thinking can change direction.
Picabia.

'If you eat everything on your plate, you can play outside for another half hour.' 'The first one to finish his sums can clean the board.'

Like many people, I used rewards to manipulate my children's behavior for a long time.

Yes, I see giving rewards to children as a form of manipulation because we use them to try to get them where we want them. This will come as a surprise to some people. These people may already see punishment as harmful: when we do it, we manipulate our children into doing what we want them to and thereby prevent them from finding out for themselves how they want to live. That rewards have the same effect is for many new, but they do. By giving a reward, I make it clear that I am the one to decide what is good: to eat everything on your plate is always good for everyone; to leave anything on it is a disgrace, a waste of valuable food and money. I, as an adult, know what's right. I put myself on a pedestal. I have an idea of what people should and shouldn't do in life and I would prefer that the people around me conform to that idea. I don't just hand out rewards for the fun of it. Consciously or unconsciously, I have an ulterior motive, namely that next time, the child receiving the reward will again behave as I wish in the hope of being rewarded again.

Perhaps you are thinking: 'That's right. Of course I know what's good for my children. I'm an adult and I'm responsible for their upbringing. If I just let my kids have their own way, there'll be chaos.' Ceasing to give rewards does not mean just letting children have their own way. We will see that there are alternatives to giving rewards. What I want to point out is that giving rewards results in the recipient feeling content about him or herself only on receiving approval from another person.

You may be one of the people who have never looked at giving rewards in this way and the paragraphs above may have aroused your curiosity. Please read further. But beware! This could alter your ideas about child-rearing completely. That's what happened to me.

When I say 'rewarding' I mean giving or promising to give something to someone if they do what I tell them: 'Because you've tidied up your room so nicely, we'll go into town and have an ice-cream.' What I have against this form of rewarding will hopefully become clear as you read this book. I do not want to throw away the *appreciation* packaged within the reward. Appreciation can always be expressed in another way: for instance 'I love the peace and quiet in your room when it's neat and tidy.' Or: 'Are you enjoying getting your room all organized?' These are messages beginning with 'I' or questions which express interest in the other. We all need acknowledgement. We like to be seen, and appreciation is a lovely way to show that we've seen somebody.

To enable children to 'grow up in trust', there are some prerequisites. For the initial period after birth, children are babies. Safe bonding with one or more nurturing adults lays an important basis for a trustful life. One of the ways this trust comes about is through offering the baby a peaceful and structured environment. However much we try to respond to the wishes of a baby, *we* still decide which clothes it will wear, what it eats, whether it goes outside and a great deal more besides. As a child gets bigger, it increasingly decides for itself what it will or will not do. During this process, we are in constant dialogue with ourselves about how much to guide and set boundaries and when to relax our control. I see this as a gradual process which begins with guiding and setting boundaries in almost everything and ends with being a supportive presence.

Instead of wanting to raise our children to be an exact copy of ourselves, we can develop trust in every child's potential for growth and self-discipline. It's about ceasing to want to play the 'boss' over our children and wanting instead to stand beside them, stimulating and supporting them.

If we work in education, are parents ourselves, or if we work or are planning to work with parents or educators in some other context, it may not be easy to make room to put this new approach into practice within our team or family.

I am the mother of three children myself. I used sometimes to be tired or run off my feet and I was occasionally strict and demanding. As a speech-therapist, I often worked with stickers and album pictures as rewards. Yet all along, something about it was bothering me. On the other hand, I also have happy memories of the times when I allowed myself to be led by and to respond to what was going on in the children or when I had discussions with them and allowed my decisions and solutions to emerge from these. However, after reading 'Nonviolent Communication' by Marshall B. Rosenberg and 'Punished by Rewards' by Alfie Kohn, I decided to hesitate no longer. I resolved to give up using rewards and punishments except for when I really couldn't think of another way of resolving a situation. Making this resolution in itself didn't take me much time or effort – and who knows, you may find yourself wanting to make the same resolution as you read this book.

If this should happen, a process of growing awareness will then begin. You will probably resort less and less to reward and punishment. You will learn about and learn to use alternatives compatible with trust and giving space. My advice would be to try them out first in situations you find relatively easy. It all takes a bit of getting used to. You wouldn't expect to be able to drive through town at rush hour after your first driving lesson after all.

I was fortunate enough to work in a one-woman speech-therapy practice and to have the sole responsibility for rearing my own children. I was free to experiment. In the meantime I have become an international Nonviolent Communication trainer.

Living without rewards or punishment is completely compatible with what I propagate. But I still feel lonely sometimes when friends, acquaintances or people I meet through my work stop listening when I tell them I think rewards and punishment are a form of manipulation. Fortunately, I also see the peace, joy and self-confidence grow in the children I respond to with empathy, interest and honesty instead of with praise and rewards.

Adults too feel comfortable with me when I don't reproach them if they fail to do what I ask of them or when I don't reward them with words of praise if they dance to my pipes. But in this book, I will concentrate on the relationships between parents and/or educators and children. Readers can draw their own conclusions with regard to relationships with adults.

The reason I am so keen to highlight the effects of giving rewards is that I know how much it affects our lives. I experience its effects myself almost every day. It would not be an exaggeration to say that I used to be 'addicted' to approval. I don't doubt that my parents really loved me and probably because they thought it was the 'right' thing to do, they expressed their love by bringing me up to be a good, hard-working person. But they did this by consistently praising me for what in their eyes would lead to the fruition of this goal and punishing me if I did anything that in their eyes would divert me away from it. The result is that I still occasionally panic when I am criticized and feel insecure if others fail to see and tell me how well I'm doing.

With the help of a number of therapists and by working on myself, I can now function reasonably well without approval. Working on this book has helped me enormously.

Perhaps you recognize some aspects of this story. I sincerely hope this book can spare some children from this pain. Wouldn't it be wonderful if children were to develop a deeply anchored feeling of self-confidence and not remain dependent on what others think of them for the rest of their lives?

In a world without rewards and punishment, our lives would change dramatically. In this world we would:

-be able to relate to the world, both inside and outside of ourselves, whole-heartedly, as we would focus on the process and not on the goal (the reward);

-be unhindered by fear of failure or missing out on a reward, so we could learn unimpeded;

-feel safe and experience the freedom to experiment;

-learn that everyone is unique and special and be free from labels and judgments;

-remain open and curious;

-remain involved if something were to go wrong and find a way to do it differently;

-not be dependent on other people's approval to feel whole.

Some people may find themselves resistant to some passages in this book. Bringing up children can sometimes be a difficult task and they may occasionally think: 'She can talk, but it's not that easy in practice.' Or they may find themselves confronted with their own shortcomings when they're not in the mood for it. If you are one of these people, it may be easier to dismiss my suggestions as being suited to another planet than to admit to yourself that what you are doing is not always fruitful.

I would like to ask you to read this book without punishing yourself for what you might conclude you are doing 'wrong'. Regard what you meet with curiosity and take a moment to register what my words do to you without judgment. I don't have a patent on the truth. During my workshops on Nonviolent Communication and Raising Kids in Trust, I always begin by saying that I'm going to place a collection of knowledge, ideas, wisdom and suggestions in the middle of the room in an imaginary bowl. And I invite the participants to take out what is useful to them, and to leave the rest where it is. I invite you to read this book in the same spirit.

'Everything worth doing is worth doing poorly.'
Marshall B. Rosenberg

1

WHY WITHOUT REWARDS AND

PUNISHMENT?

We probably all worry when our children do things of which we don't approve. We probably all think it's important that they adapt to the norms of society and that things will go amiss if they don't. There may also be practical reasons for us to want them to stop doing certain things. Sometimes it would be just downright inconvenient if they continued to do what they're doing. We'd like some peace and quiet or we're afraid that something will get broken. By punishing our children, we try to prevent undesirable behavior being repeated or to stop our children from 'being naughty'.

The result *may* be that they never repeat the behavior for which we have punished them. This however, will not flow from for instance the child's heart-felt desire to please, or because they no longer feel the need to 'be naughty', but from fear, guilt and shame. Children are afraid of being punished again. They think it is their fault that people are angry at them, so they take responsibility for other people's feelings and needs. They feel ashamed because they have done something wrong. If they continually hear that they are stupid, lazy, ungrateful and clumsy, and are punished for it, they will feel ashamed of who they are and begin to doubt themselves.

> With her ball, Wendy has flattened a row of tulips in the neighbors' front garden. As a punishment, she is not allowed to play outside for a week. When her friends ring the doorbell to ask her to come outside and play, she is

ashamed because she has done something wrong. She thinks it is her fault that the neighbors and her mum and dad are angry. When she is allowed out again, she no longer dares to play with her ball for fear that disaster will strike again.

She was probably shocked when she saw all the flattened tulips and perhaps felt very uncomfortable. She didn't need to be punished to realize that this was not what anyone wanted. With or without the intervention of an adult, she would probably have found a way of taking responsibility. She might have picked the broken tulips and taken them to the neighbors with her apologies or asked if there was something she could do for them. She might have offered to be more careful when playing with her ball in future, or to play a bit further away. There *is* a risk that it might happen again, but punishment is no sure-fire means of prevention.

Just as with punishment, rewards can also lead to fear, guilt and shame. If you are given a reward because people think you are good at something, you may get the idea that you have to continue to live up to their high expectations. You become afraid of failure, blame yourself if things don't succeed and are ashamed of your short-comings.

Gerry has written an entertaining article for the school paper. The English teacher is full of praise and he is given a regular column in the paper. The next time he *has to* write an article, he feels tense. He is afraid of disappointing the teacher. When, with great difficulty, he wrings something out of his computer, he is ashamed of the result. When his teacher is indeed disappointed, he feels guilty.

Perhaps you feel this tension too when something is expected of you. Your wife invites a few friends over to eat and asks you to cook your speciality for them. She tells her friends in voluptuous detail what a wonderful cook you are. You become nervous. You try your very best - with the result that you forget to put salt in the food and the oven-dish burns.

In my opinion, reward and punishment are forms of manipulation. Words of praise and criticism fall under the same heading. We can punish by means of beating, confining or withholding such funda-mentals as sleep or food. Blaming, disparaging remarks, and threats have the same effect. Children are afraid of them and try to avoid them by doing as they're told. We hand out rewards such as stickers, sweets, money and gifts. The result is that children do as we tell them because they want the rewards. When we say: 'Good boy' or 'That's right!', the same happens. 'Good' and 'right' are as much judgments as 'bad' and 'wrong'. If we like the drawing a child has done, he will be happy. If we don't, he will no longer take pleasure in it himself. So praise makes a child just as dependent on us as giving a concrete reward.

I use the word 'manipulation' because when we punish or reward, we try to bend our children to our will. A child is not a piece of clay to be moulded until it conforms to our ideals. By punishing or ignoring *wrongness*, and by praising or rewarding *rightness* we try to get children to behave in a certain way: our way. Children understand this readily and conclude that perhaps we only love them if they do as they're told: in other words, that our love for them is conditional.

We can let people know what we think of their actions without rewarding or punishing them: that certain behaviors detract from life (Oops, now the tablecloth is all wet) or enhance life (So, now all the milk is in your tummy). Tone of voice is of course all-important. Before we know it, an approving or disapproving tone creeps into what we are saying or we give out other non-verbal signals.

Our love for our children is not being disputed here. What we can learn to do is to mourn some sorts of behavior and celebrate others. If a child experiences his own behavior in these terms, we can mourn or celebrate together. What's important to me is to show that all behavior can be seen as a 'given', part of the learning process, and says something about the skills acquired so far and what is going on inside someone. The more I am able to accept what *is*, the more the child experiences room for growth.

Compliments can have the same effect as rewards, although they are usually meant to express something nice. What is the difference between a compliment and praise? The intention behind praise is to express approval; compliments are intended to say something nice to someone. But is there not more to them? Take the compliments other adults give to you, or those you give to them. 'You look nice', 'How brave of you to tell the boss you didn't agree with him'. How do you feel when you hear this sort of thing? Happy? Strong?

We also criticize each other. 'That coat doesn't suit you', 'You're stupid. You should keep your mouth shut'. How do you feel then? Unhappy, insecure?

In both cases, you are pretty dependent on how others think of you.

Compliments and criticism work like this because we have been damaged by living in a society in which we are constantly manipulated. When we say: 'You look nice', we usually mean: 'I like the way you look. I love that gorgeous color of blue'. The compliment says a little bit about the recipient, but a lot more about the speaker. Alas, the recipient often hears a judgment.

How has it come about that rewards play such a large role in our society? Why do we think rewards are necessary? Or that we can't be happy without rewards? Or that the world would be in a mess without them? Punishing children has taken place for centuries, and rewards are also no recent development. The 'educational' use of reward came into being around the time when B.F. Skinner (1904-1990) discovered 'operant conditioning'. During an experiment with rats, he discovered that they could be trained to lower a barrier if, behind it, a tasty morsel was placed, accessible only by doing so. In this way, the rats' actions were rewarded with the tasty morsel. He went further and applied this discovery to people and since Skinner, it has become a widely accepted means of getting people to do what we want.

However, Skinner and his followers missed one important detail. People are not animals. People can think, have a conscience and are able to make choices from freedom and inner motivation. We *can* get them to do as we want by rewarding them, but we cannot essentially change them. If we think that by rewarding them, people can develop into hard-working, socially-minded beings and simultaneously be happy and healthy, we are mistaken. It doesn't work like that.

Until recently, business communities as well as educationalists and families, have frantically sought new forms of reward which would finally work: extra perks and bonuses, a promotion, a trip with all expenses paid for the adults; and increasingly refined points systems and more and more expensive gifts such as mobile phones and dvd-players for children. But the insight is gradually dawning upon us that we can also change direction and look for alternatives. In Chapter 11, I have listed a number of these alternatives.

Here are a few reasons why rewarding is inadvisable:

-Rewards lead to competition. 'The first one to finish can wipe the board clean.' 'The person with the highest marks will get a book by J.K. Rowling.' If a child hears this, he may be less likely to want to help other kids, or to collaborate by doing sums in a group: it might take up too much time and the other kids might get higher marks if he does. Sometimes the competitive element serves to stimulate. If people can choose whether or not to participate in a competition, I have no problem with it. Whether we like it or not, as long as rewards have a place in our system, children will be exposed to it wherever they go.

-Rewards often take the place of attention for what's going on inside a child. If I promise a child who has got out of bed a few times in the evening that we'll go for a pizza tomorrow on condition that he now stays in bed, I can probably finally read my paper in peace, but I don't know what's bothering him. Is he feeling lonely there, alone in his room? Is there something he still wants to tell or ask me, before he goes to sleep? Has he got a tummy-ache?

-Rewards cause us to choose the safe, easy path. They are the enemy of the investigator in us. We do no more than is necessary to ensure our reward. We pay no attention to anything peripheral to the task at hand. We do not seek other solutions to our problems. People who are used to receiving rewards tend to get into the habit of doing as little as possible, even when the reward system is no longer operational.

-Rewards reduce our interest in a lesson's subject-matter. True attention and enthusiasm for the content of an assignment disappear. Children cheer if the school-day ends an hour earlier and they count the days till the holidays.

-In an environment where rewards are given daily, children lose their inner motivation or their 'intrinsic motivation'. The motivation to learn something unfortunately often comes from the outside world. We call this 'extrinsic motivation'. With extrinsic motivation, work is done with the sole purpose of achieving a 'pass', or gaining a certificate. Children only help around the house if they're paid for it or if they get something in exchange.

-In a system of reward and punishment, children learn nothing about cooperation, harmony and mutual respect. They do learn about domination: the person with the most power gets his or her way and those with less power have to either succumb or rebel.

In his book 'Punished by Rewards', Alfie Kohn describes amongst other things Alan Kadzin's research in the second half of the 20th century. For a period of twelve days, Kadzin handed out rewards to a group of 9-11 year old children when they played with certain arithmetical games and withheld these rewards when they played with other games. The children were told that all the games were equally interesting. They promptly fell on the games that promised a reward. But when the rewards were withheld after twelve days, their interest in these games declined markedly. In the end, the children became less interested in the games than before the prospect of rewards had been offered in the first place. The researchers concluded that powerful, systematic rewarding may result in a lowering of involvement in the task. The following example comes from the same book.

Every day, an old man was verbally abused by a group of ten-year-olds as they passed his house on their way home from school. After hearing for the umpteenth time how stupid, ugly and bald he was, he got an idea. The next day, he went and met them and announced that everyone who came next day to give him another skin-full of abuse would get a dollar. Amazed and excited, they came the next day and shouted more fanatically than ever. The man gave them each a dollar. 'If you come again tomorrow, you'll each get 50 cents,' he said. Okay, they still thought it was worth it, so next day, there was an ear-splitting racket at his door yet again. He paid up as promised but said: 'This is getting a bit expensive. If you come again tomorrow, I'll give you ten cents.' The children looked at each other. 'Ten cents? I'm not doing it for that.' And they never came back.

What the old man had done was to deflate their intrinsic

motivation. Something they had initially done with pleasure was no fun at all any more. Whether they realize it or not, this is what millions of well-intentioned parents, teachers and other educators do on a daily basis to the children they reward. By using bribery, they end up killing interest in exactly the things for which they want to stimulate interest.

PRACTICE

At the end of each chapter, I will give some exercises. I hope you will see these as suggestions of how to play around with the matter dealt with in the chapter. Please don't think you have to do them all – in fact you don't have to do any of them. Do only those you want to and feel free to alter them to suit *you*. Or do them together with somebody else. Some exercises are probably suitable to do with a class or group. Each person can do his own thing and then experiences can be shared in the group. Please use these exercises so that *you* get something out of them.

-Think of something for which your parents or other people used to consistently praise or reward you. Perhaps you were always given a sweet if you stopped crying for example. Have a look at how you deal with sadness now. Do you find it difficult to show sadness? Are there feelings of fear, guilt or shame around this subject?

-Take an exercise book or diary. Remember some moments during the last day or week when you received a reward or some praise. Write them down. What effect did these rewards have on you? Then look at the list of 'Reasons why rewards are inadvisable'. Do you recognize any of those mechanisms?

-At the end of a day or week, write down in your exercise book or diary when you rewarded or praised a child, partner or friend. See it as research – the idea is not to condemn yourself. You will probably find yourself becoming more aware of what you do. This is a necessary step before you can decide whether you would like to change any of it or not. Think of what the effects of giving this reward might be on the other person. If you find it useful, use the 'Reasons why rewards are inadvisable' list.

-I would like to invite you to bring more awareness to how you use and receive compliments. If you like, use a diary or exercise book for this too. Write down some of the compliments you have given recently and the approximate words you used. What was your intention? Did you say them because you enjoyed what someone had said or done? Or did you say them out of politeness? Or because you wanted to gain someone's favour? Be honest with yourself. And what about the compliments you received? Write down something about a situation in which you were given a compliment and the effect it had on you. Realize that these words of praise say more about the person who said them and less about you. Don't get discouraged. Stay focused on what *you* think of yourself and on how *you* feel.

2

ATTENTION

There's something that puzzles me. If I give attention to something someone does, surely I'm encouraging that behavior? If I give attention to positive behavior – sharing sweets, picking up something someone has dropped, treading softly on the stairs if someone's trying to sleep – then surely that behavior will be repeated? And if I ignore negative behavior – talking out of turn, whining for an ice-cream, teasing sisters – then surely that behavior will disappear of its own accord? My child will surely be exemplary?

Yes, that's right. It's certainly a way to produce 'exemplary' children. Marshall Rosenberg calls them 'nice dead people'. People who will be no trouble to anyone, behave nicely and never stand up for themselves: that is, for as long as they can keep it up. From time to time, they will lose control of the beast within and swear at a colleague, hurl a torrent of abuse at their partner or be unreasonably strict with their children. Occasionally, such people may actually physically abuse or even kill someone and people who know them will say: 'I just don't understand it. He/she was such a nice person: always friendly and helpful, never angry.' I'm not trying to say that all people known as friendly or calm are potential murderers, but behind that friendliness, there may hide a lot of pain. Pain and fear of showing what they really feel, fear of rejection if they don't conform to the sometimes hypocritical world around them.

Pent up aggression can also turn inwards and then these 'nice, dead people' become ill. They go through life with a conscious or unconscious fear of not being accepted if they give space to the beast within. These people are not living freely in the sense that they lack the trust and courage necessary to acknowledge what they feel and need or dare to communicate about it. They conclude that happiness is for them unattainable and resign themselves to a life full of limitations.

What about your upbringing? Perhaps *your* desirable behavior was encouraged too, and your undesirable behavior rejected? The people who brought you up probably made some fairly arbitrary decisions about what was desirable or undesirable. I don't intend this as an indictment of our loving and well-intentioned parents or other involved adults. They were no doubt influenced by the spirit of their times and had our best interests at heart. And we in turn are marked by our upbringing as we bring up our own children. Most of us swear from time to time that we will do it differently from how *our* parents and teachers did it. But this is easier said than done. Established patterns tend to be stubborn and changing them demands patience. In this context, I want to talk about the Japanese word 'kaizen'. It means: small, apparently insignificant, continuous, never-ending progress. This word gives me comfort and the courage to go on, even at those moments when I'm suffering from the patterns I seem to be so utterly stuck in that I can't move a centimeter. I wish you 'kaizen' too.

But let's get back to attention and compliant behavior. One of the dangers about ignoring undesirable behavior is of ignoring the reason why the child is behaving in this way in the first place and the underlying unfulfilled needs. I think it's important that children are told about the effects of their behavior on others. Let children know that pinching hurts, that their screaming is bothering us. Or turn it around and ask them if they'd like to stroke us instead of pinching us and tell them we enjoy hearing their voices more if they speak more softly. I wouldn't recommend repeating this information. We would then be encouraging undesirable behavior by giving attention to it – the very mechanism we want to avoid. Once should be enough.

The most important thing is what we say afterwards. After telling a child the effect of his or her behavior or what behavior we prefer, it's important to pay attention to what's bothering him.

And we can assume that something is bothering the child or he wouldn't be whining or uncooperative. We could interpret this behavior as the child saying 'no' to something. The pinching or screaming means: 'No, I don't want........'. The problem may be something going on in the child's life, but it may also be something pressing from within the child. She may for instance not be sure if she will be invited to her friend's birthday party, or she may have the first symptoms of 'flu'. It's often something that the child herself is not aware of, which is not so strange, as I myself often don't immediately know what's bothering me when I'm irritable or off-hand. If I go and sit down quietly, it will usually become clear. Sometimes it helps me to find out if someone else asks me questions. Most children appreciate getting this sort of help from adults.

If we can see a child's behavior as saying 'no' to something, it's useful when having this sort of conversation to find out what the child is saying 'yes' to. Try to find out what he needs in order to feel good again.

This assistance doesn't always have to be given in the form of talking. But if you do want to talk about it, find an opportune moment when both you and the child have the time and space to talk. What you can also do is try to imagine what might be troubling the child or (to give him more space), empathize with the fact that *something* is troubling him. Instead of seeing a whining, uncooperative child, you see a child who isn't happy and is expressing it in a bothersome way.

Steven has two daughters who sometimes fight like vixens. Particularly in the car. He no longer even hears what the row is about. He ignores their pushing and pulling and concentrates on the road. As soon as it's quiet in the back, he starts up a conversation. He tells them something about his work and asks them questions about school. The rest of the trip is usually amiable. He's perfectly content about this. The kids are never troublesome for long with him. Yes, he knows how to handle these situations.

At a certain point, he comes home one evening, and finds the house in chaos. The youngest daughter has had a temper tantrum and trashed her sister's room. She has sustained a bloody wound to her hand in the process. She then shut herself up in her own room. His wife and eldest daughter are totally flabbergasted and are considering ringing the doctor or the police.

Steven realizes that underlying his daughters' arguments, there is perhaps a drama that he was as yet unaware of.

There are various ways to live with what's hidden behind undesirable behavior. Children sometimes just enjoy being grouchy without having to explain themselves. We can show we understand that something is troubling them by giving them a bit of space and for instance, clearing the table even if it is his turn. I remember my son almost never used to get angry. When he did occasionally lose his temper, I kept his two sisters away from him and allowed him to erupt in peace. That too was a way of giving attention to what was going on behind his behavior without interfering or psychologizing.

My son wasn't one to talk about his feelings and experiences anyway. I can still envision myself sitting on his bed in an attempt to make contact with him. I asked him one question after another, none of which he answered. I now think he was just waiting for me to finish and leave him in peace. At a certain point, he said: 'Mum, couldn't you put all those questions into one question. We'd be finished much quicker.'

You can read more about where to direct your attention in Chapter 9: Hearing the 'yes' in a child's 'no'.

PRACTICE

- For this, you need one or more other people. Everyone writes down a number of examples of what they would call undesirable behavior. Talk about this with each other. Look at the differences without judging anything. It doesn't matter whether you describe undesirable behavior in adults or children

- Choose an example of what you would call undesirable behavior you have come across in someone recently. What might have been troubling that person? It doesn't matter whether you are right. The point is to empathize.
- How do you behave if something is troubling you? Do you withdraw? Do you become a nag? What do you do?

- Make time to sit down quietly. Get yourself something to drink, put on some music. Think about what conforming or compliant behavior of yours no longer suits you. Think of situations when you exhibit this behavior. How do others react to it? How do *you* feel when you do it? Would you have the courage to behave differently in those situations from now on? If the answer is yes, think of how you would like to behave instead. Sit yourself down once or twice a week to evaluate. How is it going? Are you succeeding in behaving differently? What do you gain from it? What is the response from people who know you and are unused to this new behavior from you?

3

BASIC NEEDS

All over the world, children need to learn and play. But this is not all. They want to decide for themselves what they do and they want to be treated with love and respect. It would be true to say that they have a whole list of basic needs and only when these are fulfilled are they truly happy. Needs such as food and drink, warmth and sleep belong to this list too. Adults have the same basic needs, but the way they prefer to have them satisfied is sometimes different. Once we discover that there are various ways of meeting the same needs we can find ways for different people to meet their needs in harmony with one another. When needs or best interests differ, it is also possible to arrange things in such a way that everyone is happy. It is then a question of choosing strategies which don't interfere with others getting their needs met too. It's worth trying to do this before resorting to rewards or punishment to ensure that we at least will get our needs met. Or before we go to the other extreme of offering ourselves up for our children's happiness, and finding ourselves exhausted at the end of the day.

Giving the same weight to each person's needs and best interests may seem a little roundabout at first. And it does take time, especially as we take our first wobbly steps. But the result is that we stand a good chance of satisfying everyone. If each member of the family consistently takes the others' needs seriously, we will soon notice that meeting each other's needs seems to be much more enjoyable than it used to be.

Martin (9), Sophie (12) and their parents all need some peace and quiet. Martin loves laying out his Lego on the floor and playing with it for hours. Sophie likes watching and listening to video-clips of her favourite bands on TV. Their mother likes the house to be neat and tidy and their father wants to read the paper in peace (and quiet). Their needs are the same, but they each have their own way of meeting it. This sometimes results in heated rows always ending with either parents or children getting the short end of the stick. Putting their trust in this new phenomenon, 'basic needs', they decide to sit down at the table together and look for a solution which will provide each member of the family with the peace and quiet he or she is seeking. And it turns out that there are all sorts of possibilities: Martin can for instance, sit in his own room. Sophie can use head-phones. Or Dad can go and sit somewhere else if there aren't any head-phones. Or they can agree on a time for Sophie to watch TV, while Dad postpones his peace and quiet. Martin can divide off an area of the room with his Lego bricks so Mum can keep the rest of the room neat and tidy. So there are all sorts of ways to meet everyone's needs.

Do you recognize the following scenario? You've slept well, and you're enjoying your work or the company of the people you live with. Taking others into account and setting your boundaries comes easily to you.

And do you recognize this? You're tired, your work is stressful and the house is a mess. You work yourself to the bone and are irritated by everything and everyone.

Could it be that it is easier to be there for others if we first take care of ourselves? Recently, I notice more and more how good it feels, in amongst the hubbub of the day, to take a moment for myself - lie down for half an hour in my bed, take a walk down to the post-box, ring a friend, take the time to do my Qi Cong exercises.

This 'first me, then the others' idea was affirmed during an air trip I took recently. As part of the standard safety instructions, they emphasized that in case of emergency, we should fit our own oxygen masks first before those of our children. In other words, take care of ourselves first, because if we don't, we may not be able to take care of our children at all.

Taking care of ourselves can also mean recognizing our needs. Sometimes, there really isn't much opportunity to do anything about getting our needs met, and then recognizing them and for instance, taking a couple of deep breaths is better than nothing. Perhaps there will be an opportunity later in the day. In Chapter 10, extensive attention is paid to caring for ourselves.

For adults, it can be very tempting to decide how our children are to behave. After all, adults have experience of life, don't they? They are better able to foresee the effects of certain actions. To protect children from danger, surely it is better to use rewards and punishment? In my opinion, no. Children's basic needs get left out that way. But it can be difficult to see it from this standpoint if we've never done it before. So let's go into a number of these basic needs to get a clearer view.

The need for security
In the introduction on page 3, I wrote about secure bonding and babies. Security remains important to children of all ages, in the sense of 'having permission to be' with all their quirks and imperfections; knowing they will be taken care of and that they will be protected if necessary. In other words, children feel secure if they know they are loved unconditionally.

The need for autonomy
It appears that children of our times, more so than in the past, want to decide for themselves how, what and when they will learn. They will not be coerced. They are clever. If we do try to force them to do anything, they will think up all sorts of ways of getting out of it. Of course, they can't do everything alone yet, and they need

help, whether with putting on their socks or with writing a letter. They enjoy learning things from us, but only when they choose to. They like to choose the manner in which they learn, too.

The need for authenticity
Each child is unique and seeks ways of learning and developing which suit him or her. It's worth bearing this in mind when a child indicates that it wants to do something on its own. Isn't it wonderful, watching a small child putting food onto his spoon with one hand in order to put the spoon into his mouth with the other? Or watching an eight-year-old discover his own method of doing a sum with even bigger numbers? Be careful about steering. It often smothers creativity. And children will tend towards dependant behavior if they notice that you always know better anyway.

The need for recognition
People like to be seen and to be taken seriously: children too. I remember when I was a child, that I blossomed when people saw my shyness and showed me some consideration. Like the time I arrived at a friend's birthday party, and an adult smiled at me, then without needing to gently took me by the shoulder and guided me to a chair at a corner of the table from where I could quietly take in all the festivities and gradually get used to it all.

The need for respect
Children like to have their autonomy and authenticity respected. So if we decide that the table must be cleared NOW because we want it laid for the meal, we can say something like: 'What a shame – just when you'd like to play for a bit longer.'

Respect doesn't mean letting someone have their own way. It has more to do with honouring them. What you are really saying inside is: 'I have regard for your wish to continue to draw at the table a bit longer. I love you, even at times when you don't immediately do what I want you to.'

Besides this, we can practice acceptance: accepting that everything exists. It doesn't mean we respect everything. I respect that a child gets angry, but I do not accept his smashing glasses. I intervene to stop it.

The need for empathy

We can empathize by listening with love, giving recognition and by understanding. When doing this, we need to avoid judgements, comparisons, generalizations and solutions. They only get in the way of empathy.

If we are empathizing with a success someone has had, it may take the form of showing that we value something. If something hasn't worked out, we can give it our attention for a moment and show our regret. When I say 'showing we value something', I don't mean we have to say: 'Well done'. That just renders people insecure and dependant. I mean we can show we enjoyed someone's actions, manner or words. If a six-year-old girl has pumped up her bicycle's tyres, instead of saying 'Well done', we might express our joy at the fact that she is getting bigger and more independent. We might say: 'I see you've pumped the tyres up all by yourself. You're glowing with pride. I'm happy because it means you won't be needing my help with that any more. It's nice, being able to do things yourself, isn't it?' This could also be said with fewer or no words at all. The same message might be communicated by putting an arm round her shoulder and smiling into her eyes, accompanied with 'Great, huh?' If we are thinking 'Well done,' it will still come over as a reward. So it's not only about what we say or do, it's also about the intention of showing that we value something.

For the last two years, I have babysat the little girl next door one day a week. She is now three. Instead of : 'Well done!' I have trained myself to say 'You did it!' And if she upsets a glass of juice, I say: 'Oh dear!' or 'What a pity.' In this way, I empathize with what is going on in her. She is happy if something works and is regretful if something falls over. I don't need to underline it for her by overwhelming her with words of praise or criticism. More about this in Chapter 5.

The need for equality

Children are capable of discovering for themselves where their qualities lie and how they want to develop them. We need to get down off our pedestals and communicate with our children! Adults and children can learn a lot from each other. I have in mind a boy of ten, very sensitive to what's going on in other people. It overwhelms him a bit. He is curious and wants to be able to do something for other people, but he also finds it a bit scary. He doesn't play with other children a lot. If we were his parents, would we decide that it was time he came out of his isolation and would we decide for him how he should do it? Would we take him to the field behind the school when there are other kids playing football in the hope that he'll make friends? Would we invite his classmates to come and play with him at home?

We might also go and talk to the boy to find out what he feels ready for. We could ask him questions, ask if he'd like us to think along with him. We could see him as an equal partner in the conversation. Children like to be seen as a whole, not a half. At each age, and with each child, equality takes on a different meaning. There can be equality even in the contact with babies. They are real human beings with their own feelings and needs and their own way of communicating them. It's up to us to get onto the same wave-length. We just need to keep searching.

The need for loving attention

Children have a powerful longing for unconditional love, whatever they do. They don't only want loving attention when they have done something good in our eyes. When I was on holiday in Ireland, I saw a sign hanging on a wall which read: 'We need loving the most when we deserve it the least'.

The need for play and learning

Suppose we are going to do some drawing with a child of 2½ and we're going to use blocks of coloured beeswax. We start to draw. The child also puts a few lines on his paper and then starts investigating the wax blocks themselves. She builds a tower with them.

She takes them out of the box, then puts them back in again, trying to get them to fit. She scratches one with her nail so that little bits of wax come off. Suppose we immediately try to teach her 'what the blocks are for'. We praise her when she draws and ignore her when she does anything else. Or we say: 'No, that's not what the blocks are for'. We would be depriving her of an opportunity to play and learn.

If she starts drawing on the table or on her clothes, we could quietly take her arm and bring it back to the paper. We could be clear and decisive: 'No. I don't want the table (or your sweater) to get dirty.' We don't get angry, we don't punish her.

Children like to experiment and they are more likely to be prepared to do so within our boundaries if they're accustomed to us respecting their boundaries too. We might say that children challenge us to play with our boundaries.

The need for humor and pleasure

Like adults, children are more likely to take others into account when they are having fun: a joke, a wink, a friendly tussle, shared laughter. When my kids were at puberty, I could sometimes be very serious and uncompromising. If they didn't put their dirty clothes in the washing basket, I didn't wash them. If I found clothes on the floor, I'd nag them about it. In this way, not having their clothes washed was experienced as a punishment and having them washed, as a reward. I would even take pleasure in the fact that there was no clean shirt for my son when he wanted to leave for the football pitch. 'It's your own fault', I thought, 'you should have put it in the washing basket.'

Looking back, I realize that this was my way of trying to fulfill my need for rest and order. I now know that it was a tragic way, because the repetitive arguments about dirty washing didn't bring me any rest or order at all. In other words, this punishment and reward did not produce the desired result. A well-placed remark such as 'Great! The wash-basket is still empty. I don't have to do a wash today' or a temporary campaign of arrows marked 'Washing this Way' all over the house have far more chance of success. A pleasant side-effect is that if I don't get myself so wound up any more, my need for rest is already fulfilled.

More basic needs are listed in Marshall B. Rosenberg's book 'Nonviolent Communication'. I hope the message is now clear. Children's basic needs are not fulfilled by our punishing or rewarding them. When we pay attention to the basic needs of the children we interact with, we will keep finding that we need to look for other means to fulfill these needs. In my experience, this is very difficult if I don't know which needs are behind my own irritation or nagging. So I would recommend looking at our own needs first and meeting them if we can. If at a given moment, we can see no way of doing so, we can be compassionate to our own pain and sadness about things going differently from how we would like them to. If we take good care of ourselves, we will have far more patience with the children entrusted to our charge.

PRACTICE

- Take a look at the needs described in this chapter. Do any of these needs ring a bell? Take a moment to think about them or talk to someone else about them. When does a certain need get met, and when not? Can you fulfill the need yourself, or do you always need others to do it? How do you feel when the need is met? How do you behave if it isn't met?

By thinking about it in this way, we become familiar with the fact that we have basic needs and with their significance in our lives.

-Think of your own child or another child you know well. Remember a moment when you thought this child was being troublesome or a nuisance. Did you attempt to rein him/her in with a punishment or reward? How did it end? Go back again now to the point at which the child was troublesome. Sit down and give yourself the time to think about what unmet needs might have been at play.

-There are other basic needs such as the need for trust, protection, support, clarity, wholeness, safety, making a contribution towards the happiness of others. Perhaps you can think of still more.
Read the situations below and try to identify the needs screaming for attention. Pick the sentences with which you feel an affinity.

- The teacher is explaining something to Karen. Karen is not looking at her and starts chattering.

- Richard starts shouting and swearing when Pete borrows his pen for a moment without asking.

- Sasha never tidies up her room, even though her mother asks her to almost every day.

- Steve just will not remain seated at the table.

- Katinka has been sitting staring out of the window all morning.

- The teacher has set the class to work. Julie still wants to ask something and raises her hand. She always does that.

- Patrick is walking home through the park. He rips off a couple of leaves from each bush he passes.

4

CHILDREN'S BUILT-IN MORALITY

Parents and educators tend to worry about their children or the children entrusted to them. Are they learning enough? Do they have enough friends? Do they take others into consideration? Are they troublesome to others? Motivated by these concerns, it occurs to many of us that we as adults have a responsibility to teach our children consideration, empathy and helpfulness. And when a child suddenly puts an arm around someone who is crying or gives a toy away because another child wants it so badly, this is seen as a sign that we have brought them up well. And we take refuge in authoritarian methods to ensure and prolong this altruistic behavior.

Rudof Steiner (and with him, the German psychologist, Henning Köhler) said there is no reason to worry and that our intervention is unnecessary. He emphasized that children are naturally attracted to moral behavior. If they are given the space to develop it, and if parents and teachers set a good example of socially conscious behavior, all will be well according to him. It is important that parents be living examples. That's not what's under discussion here.

Children up to the age of seven learn largely through imitation. If children experience violence or lack of respect in their surroundings, this is what they will imitate. This goes against their inborn tendency towards morality and can even supersede it. We make it easier for them by giving them an example of moral living. This means, amongst other things, empathizing with others, being considerate and helpful, not judging, but showing genuine interest in the way other people choose to live. And by 'other people', I don't mean only adults, but also our own and others' children.

Any attempt to 'instill' morality into children will have the opposite effect. It will actually get in the way of the child developing his own independent morality and ultimately, his own independent ideals. A feeling of sympathy for all that is 'good' is not stimulated by upbringing, but comes from within. Just take a look at the way a child's eyes shine in response to his parents 'good deeds'. Children do not react with pride to meanness in their parents.

Three girls have been best friends since their first year at primary school. Their friendship is anything but boring. Sometimes one of them will be sad because she thinks the other two are excluding her. Another time, they'll have the whole class against them because they won't let anyone else into their tightly-knit group. When one of them wants to celebrate her fifteenth birthday with a party in the garden on the very day that the other two want to go to a unique pop festival, they talk about it for hours. None of the three is happy if the other two aren't. Sometimes it gets too much for one of the parents and she tries to butt in. 'What is it *you* want? Stand up for yourself!' They listen politely and then take none of it on board. It would appear that they have chosen each other to help each other to search for their own morality in this friendship.

You may find yourself thinking about an occasion when your child didn't want to share a toy and hit a child who wanted to take it. Where's the inborn morality in that? This needs explaining.

Children don't always want to take others into account. In this, they're just like adults. They want autonomy too and this can sometimes be diametrically opposed to their desire for harmony and respect. We can help children to find ways of dealing with opposing needs. It isn't easy to stand up for yourself at the same time as taking the wishes of another person into consideration.

Children generally enjoy receiving gifts. This is true. And their greed is definitely aroused by the extravagance they are exposed to almost daily in shops and on television. One of the questions that worry parents and teachers is whether children aren't too greedy, wanting to keep everything for themselves. I can reassure them. Look at how a child's eyes shine when he gives you a drawing or when she offers you a cup of tea from her doll's tea service and sees how pleased you are. This still happens when they get older. I notice each year at Sinterklaas, (Dutch holiday celebrated on 5th December) that my grown-up children and I too are far more concerned about how our gifts and poems will be received than we are curious about what we will receive ourselves. At moments such as this, the basic need to contribute to the happiness of others comes to the fore. Marshall Rosenberg puts it like this: 'The greatest joy is the joy we have in other people's joy.'

If we leave the development of morality to our children, we need patience and restraint. We first need to see what comes from the child itself and not be too quick to preach. This means having trust and giving space. A child needs time to develop this inborn morality. Beside the moral example set by the adults around him, he also comes into contact with violence from adults, on the street and on television. It isn't easy to find your own direction in this confusion or indeed to trust it once you have it.

Giving space means that we accept that every child is as he or she is. Each child, each person is unique. We can never bring children up to be a copy of ourselves.

Can we accept children with their lack of awareness, their quirks, their headstrong ways and their lack of concern? We don't have to be happy about their behavior and attitude. We are perfectly entitled to tell them what we would like. As long as we don't try to change them. Learning, arriving at new insights, growing up are things they can only do for themselves. At most, we can offer them suggestions. It is up to them whether they accept them or use them.

When my younger daughter was eight, I discovered that with her friends, she was reading magazines for which I thought she was too young. After reading an example myself, I told her I'd seen articles on subjects which might shock her or which she couldn't understand yet, and which might confuse her. She said she 'just liked' the magazine and that I needn't worry. I asked her not to buy it any more, or if she saw it somewhere, not to read it any more. I would prefer it that way. So I didn't give her the impression she had done something wrong and I didn't punish her by tearing up the magazine or taking her pocket money away if I noticed her with the same magazine in her hands again. I also didn't reward her with another magazine if she promised not to look at the first one for another three years. I respected her curiosity and her urge for sensation and excitement and told her clearly what I thought about it. I no longer remember what happened. I let go of it at that point. I think I saw the magazine in the house again once or twice, but perhaps the novelty wore off. It may be that my words and attitude set her thinking. Children really are open to the knowledge and wisdom of the adults with whom they have a bond. The more freedom and space they have, the more they will open their hearts and recognize their own wisdom in the wisdom around them.

PRACTICE

-Below is a list of twenty qualities. Not in the sense of static labels you have or have not, but more in the sense of talents you have developed in the course of your life. You will probably recognize all of them, but which of them are you fairly sure you have developed more than other talents? If you tick 'tolerant' for example, in which circumstances do you find it easy to tolerate something unpleasant without complaining and when do you find it difficult? Have you developed this quality by following the example set to you by one of your parents? Did you get a reward if you behaved in this way or were you punished for being intolerant? Does this influence the way you feel when you employ this quality now?

helpful	courageous
unpretentious	neat
trustworthy	tactful
grateful	faithful
respectful	responsible
fair	tolerant
flexible	forgiving
patient	generous
loyal	truthful
compassionate	caring
honest	considerate

- Picture a child you know well. Which of the above qualities do you consider to be obviously present in this child? What do you think? Do these qualities come from the child himself? Is she following the example of her parents (yourself, perhaps)? Is it conditioned behavior? Or is it a mixture of all of these? How can you tell?

-Is there a quality that is obviously present in yourself – caring for instance – that you would really like the children around you to develop too? How have you handled that up until now? Would you like to handle it differently? How?

5

RULES AND AGREEMENTS

What are rules for? Can a society function without rules? If someone breaks a rule, should they be punished? Lots of questions. Let's see if we can find some answers.

We have rules and we have agreements. To me, these are two completely different things, but I notice that the two words are frequently used interchangeably. For instance: 'Why haven't you done the washing up? Surely we had an agreement?' can mean: 'Surely I said you had to do the washing up – and now you haven't done it!' With this subtext, I would definitely not call this an agreement, but a demand. If your son had offered or at least agreed to do the washing up today and he hasn't done it, then indeed, he has not done what you both agreed.

I think we can speak of an agreement when all parties involved have been consulted on the possibilities and when all parties have agreed to the final decision. The difference with a rule is that it is determined by one or more persons for a larger group of people. The other members of the group have not been consulted about the instigation of the rule.

In our society, we need rules. A clear example is traffic regulations. It's useful to know from which side traffic has priority. This rule is meant to create clarity and safety. Wouldn't it be wonderful if everyone were to keep to the traffic regulations? Unfortunately, they don't always do so. So we try to avoid accidents, for instance, if a car is coming from the left (in a country where people drive on the right), by keeping our foot above the brake-pedal just in case the driver doesn't give way. This then becomes a rule we learn during our driving lessons.

Traffic violations are punished with fines and even imprisonment. Does the threat of prison influence your driving behavior?
Or would you keep the traffic rules without the threat of fines or
imprisonment? And why? Or do you make a game of not getting
caught and lose sight of the intention (preserving safety) behind
the rules? That's the way it works with me. I keep to the maximum
speed limit where there's surveillance, but otherwise, I'll allow my
speed to depend on a number of other factors. If it's quiet on the
road, I'll drive at about 130 km per hour (about 80 mph). If I'm
tired or have someone next to me who doesn't feel safe at that
speed, 100 km per hour (about 60 mph) is fine too or if it's misty or
slippery on the road. I have a strong desire for autonomy but it's
also important to me that both I and others get home safely.

On German motorways, there are stretches where you're not
allowed to drive faster than 100 km per hour. I thought this was
ridiculous until someone told me that there are residential areas
right beside these stretches and cars which drive more slowly
make less noise and produce less air pollution. Since I heard that,
I've been very careful about keeping to the maximum speed limit
there. If my motivation comes from within, I find it easier to stick
to rules.

We might describe a fine as motivation from the external world
- an attempt to force us to stick to a rule. So we obediently drive at
120 km per hour because we don't feel like being punished. Or if
we take another context: a child decides not to cheat during an
exam for fear of being punished with a low mark. I would far
rather that the child were to decide not to cheat because she's
curious about how well she'll do on her own. Or that looking at her
neighbor's paper were allowed (for instance to compare his
answers with her own) and not punished.

OK, children need rules, it's true. I'm a proponent of a non-
authoritarian upbringing. Not in the sense of letting them sort it
out themselves and do what they like, but I don't think children
should do as I say just because I'm the boss. Children need clarity.
If they know their boundaries, they will feel safe. They know what
to expect, and that gives a sense of peace. With young children, we

give this clarity by making choices for them in some cases e.g. which cup they will drink out of. Sometimes it's important to explain things to them, such as why we don't want them to put their hands in the toilet bowl after peeing. With older children, we can say clearly what we want and what we value. It's important to stay in contact with a child when we do this and watch to see how he reacts to our words and actions. Before we know it, we can start doling out reproaches, because it gives us a bit of peace and quiet. A certain amount of alertness is required to counteract this.

Instigating rules has everything to do with power. Marshall Rosenberg makes a distinction between 'punitive force' and 'protective force'. With punitive force, we make a judgment about something. We think something ought not to be done and by punishing the doer, we try to prevent it from happening again. With protective force, we intervene when danger is threatening. If a child wants to cross the road, and we see that a car is coming, we grab him by the arm and pull him back to the pavement, thereby protecting him from an accident. If we grab his arm harder than is necessary and say: 'I told you to look out! Can't you see there's a car coming!' then we are adding punishment to our protection.

Whether we are exercising protective force or not is sometimes hard to tell. My criterion for 'protective force' is force used when we are meeting certain of a child's basic needs and are convinced that he would be unable to do it for himself in this particular case. We might give a child a particular seat in the classroom for certain lessons because we have noticed that there is otherwise, no order in class. For some subjects, order is a prerequisite for learning. That's how we see it, anyway. Or perhaps we see the situation with the wisdom of experience. We might also just be sick and tired of the hullabaloo about who's allowed to sit where. We can be conscious that we are also protecting our own peace and quiet. Being conscious of why we instigate rules and of their effect on children's inner motivation can help us to be more selective in our use of force when teaching or bringing children up.

I have discovered that rules instigated from on high, when there is no respectful link between all the parties involved, can only be enforced with constant 'policing': punishment and reward. Children are far more likely to keep rules if they can understand the point of them. This doesn't mean that we always have to explain everything. If we take pupils seriously and remain open to what's going on with them at all times, they will trust that what we ask will be reasonable. Sometimes it's just nice to do what someone asks of you. You can keep your attention on something else.

We can makes rules with children from about the age of three, though if this is done together with the child, I would not call them rules, but agreements.

Teenagers need something to kick against and the boundaries we delineate in our rules are perfect for this purpose. If these boundaries are like walls with no flexibility whatever, and so high that we can no longer see each other, grim situations can result. Two camps are formed with no communication between them. We could look at boundaries as fences with which we mark off the limits of our garden. We can still see and hear our neighbors. The boundary is clearly visible but at the same time, flexible. We can make a gate so the fence can be opened sometimes. We can discuss whether there are situations in which we wouldn't mind if the fence were climbed over. We can also move it if circumstances change. The important thing is that contact remains possible.

Suppose we, a mother and father, have decided that our family will remain quietly seated at table during mealtimes and that the children will not interrupt mummy and daddy when they are having a conversation. Our son of five is still breaking this rule daily. We have punished him by seating him on his own, and rewarded him by allowing him back if he promises to behave himself. We hoped he would realize that he got more out of conforming to our rules than out of messing around. He continued to leave the table without asking, acting the clown, breaking things and playing with his food. We may ask ourselves the following. When we made the rule, we were thinking of our own peace and harmony. Did we examine whether this rule would fulfill our son's needs as well? Perhaps he needs contact, intimacy and attention, particularly at table. We could try seeing how he behaves if we start the meal with a prayer or an old saying, then consider with him what he might put on his bread and give him the chance to tell something about his school-day or friends. If he gets the feeling that his wishes matter, the chances are that he will stop continually seeking attention. He will discover that we love him, even if we are having a conversation with each other, while he sits and eats quietly. If this is not the result, we can continue the search. Can we adjust our aim of 'peace and quiet at table' to 'creating an atmosphere which everyone enjoys'? The solution may be to direct our full attention to the children while we eat. They will have the freedom to leave the table when they have finished eating, leaving us to enjoy a quiet conversation afterwards. There suddenly seem to be all sorts of possibilities if we are prepared to let go of the idea that 'we must make sure our children keep the rules by punishing and rewarding them'.

To go back to the image of the garden fence: sometimes we really don't want a fence between ourselves and our children, so we throw the gate open, so we can all sit on the grass together. As we might do if for instance we have had enough of playing policeman during mealtimes and want to explore whether we can come to some agreements with each other. We tell each other what is important to us. The person who has cooked would like to see the food he or she has prepared with love and care eaten within about half-an-hour because otherwise it will get cold. And we also want to be together each day so we can tell each other what has been happening to us. Small children may enjoy having something next to their plates to play with. As parents, we can judge whether this will contribute to the restful atmosphere at table or not. Or the child might sit on the ground beside us, playing quietly and enjoying being with us in this way. Children are unlikely to tell us that they enjoy the warm surroundings offered by a shared meal, but they do experience it. Older children can of course, speak for themselves. They may want time to finish off what they are doing, so enjoy being able to come to the table a few minutes later without it being an issue. We need to keep looking until we've found a way to satisfy everyone. This doesn't always need to come about as a result of talking. Particularly with young children, we can try things out in practice and see what works the best. We need to remember that it's all about meeting the needs of everyone concerned.

Who knows, you may decide you don't want to organize every mealtime in the same way. By letting go of the conviction: 'children should remain seated at table', creativity has room for movement. If agreements have been made, don't enter into discussion again about the first minor detail. No, an agreement is an agreement. If someone doesn't keep to the agreement, one of the others, whether adult or child can remind them of the agreement with a request: 'Would you stay sitting at table? I haven't finished eating yet.' Or use a joke or just a reminder. All without accusation, not even in the tone used to say it. If agreements are disregarded more often than you care for, look again together at what's needed and if necessary, adjust the agreement.

Praising children because they stay sitting quietly at table will no longer be necessary. They won't stay seated because we praise them. They will stay because that's what we have chosen to do, together.

While you have been reading the above, were you thinking: 'It all just takes up too much time'? Let me tell you that the investment of time during negotiations is earned back with interest later. When it is once clear that mealtimes be run to everyone's satisfaction, this no longer requires attention. How much time do you suppose you spend now on thinking up and carrying out means of keeping your children at the table? Besides, I think it's much more fun to discuss things together than to play the policeman.

PRACTICE

- How do you behave around rules? When do you have difficulty adhering to a rule and when not? Talk to other people about this. What do you think is needed to be able to live with certain rules, but without reward and punishment?

-Is there a rule you had difficulty with as a child? What would you now like to say to your parents or teachers about this rule and your resistance to it? You might try a role-play, having this conversation with the parent or adult who tried to impose this rule on you.

- Take a good look at the rules in force in your house or at work. Choose one that has been determined from on high (either by you or by someone else) and which you think could fairly easily be converted into a mutual agreement. Invite the parties involved to a meeting, tell them you are reading this book and that you'd like to talk together with them about rules. Tell them you have chosen a rule you'd like to look at together with them, because you don't like the fact that one person determines how others must behave.
    See what unfolds.

-Imagine the ideal family. Would it have rules and if so, what rules? Perhaps you'd like to write them down. You could do this exercise with the ideal school, nursery or children's department of a hospital. You could do it with any place where children are being 'raised' in any sense at all.

6

DO 'RIGHT' AND 'WRONG' (OR 'GOOD' AND 'BAD') EXIST?

'Out beyond ideas of wrongdoing and rightdoing,
there is a field. I'll meet you there.'
Rumi (Coleman Banks' translation)

These days, I often read or hear that 'right' and 'wrong' do not exist. I have thought about this and exchanged ideas with friends. If we say one and one is two, surely that's right and if we say anything else, it's wrong? Most people would agree with this. But there will always be one person who, with a grave face, will say: 'Well, not always. We recently turned two small bedrooms into one big one, so in that case, one and one was one.'

There are things most people would call 'right' or 'good'. It's a 'good' idea for example to lock the night-latch on the front door before going to bed. Although... I forgot to do so recently, and my son, who lives in another town, came home unexpectedly in the middle of the night. The next morning, he said: 'It's a good thing the night-latch wasn't locked, or I'd have had to wake you all up with the doorbell.'

The words 'good', 'bad', 'right' and 'wrong' all express a judgement.

In some situations, I have no difficulty with right and wrong. Sometimes these words offer clarity, because some things are just good or bad however you look at them.

If a child wants to draw a square and starts off with an angle of 100 degrees, it will never be a square. Making mistakes fulfills a function. We can learn from our mistakes. Whether someone tells this child that a square always has four angels of 90 degrees, whether he looks it up in a book or whether he discovers it for himself, he will always be wiser from his mistake. Because a dark cloud has come to hang over the word 'wrong', I prefer to use the word 'mistake' or 'mistaken'.

My difficulty is that we say right/wrong, good/bad, smart/stupid, should/shouldn't when *we think* it is so. 'You should finish school.' 'Reading in bed when your parents think you're sleeping is bad.' When we voice such judgements, we imply that we have the copyright on truth. We deny others the space to think otherwise.

It is different when we 'pack' our judgements in messages beginning with 'I' in which we honestly express our truth or preference (we do make judgements anyway). We say what we think of something and then link it with a request. 'I think it would be better if you finished school. Would you have another think about it?'

The words 'right' and 'wrong' got their present connotations when we started *rewarding* right and *punishing* wrong. These connotations become more loaded when we get confused between what *is* right and wrong and what *we think* is right and wrong. The result of this link between right/reward and wrong/punishment is that we walk around with a big head when we have done something 'good' and wish we could drop through a hole in the ground when we have done something 'wrong'. How would it be to replace these words with others for the time being? Then we can get used to the idea that the world does not come to an end if we do something wrong. By 'wrong' I mean something unintentional or which didn't have the desired effect.

I was at a party recently where a woman with an accordion was trying to teach the guests a dance. She began by saying that there are no such things as a mistakes, only variations. This relieved the tension. There was no 'I can't dance' or 'I've done it wrong again, I'm so stupid'. We leapt about being creative with the dance steps. In the end, we had great fun and everyone laughed at all the different 'variations'.

Marshall Rosenberg uses the terms 'life enriching' and 'life alienating' for the ways in which we communicate with each other. To tell someone: 'You always come too late. You just don't care that someone else is waiting for you, you selfish idiot!', we would first have to be alienated from life, have shut ourselves off from the fact that the other person is a human being with feelings. We would first have to see the person as an object having no relation to ourselves before we could shout at him without caring how that might be for him. It may be that later, when we have returned to our senses (the expression itself indicates that we must have been alienated from ourselves), we realize how painful the situation was.

With a question like: 'How is it that you're later than we agreed?', we make a link with what's going on in the other. We are doing something to enrich life in the sense that it has a stimulating effect. We accept the other as he or she is and show interest in what prevented him or her from being on time.

In other words: put yourself in the shoes of the other before you criticize him or her. If the other person gets the impression that he or she is seen, he will be more likely to listen to your criticism.

Here's another alternative for right and wrong. In Rosenberg's books, there are some multiple-choice exercises. In the answers, he writes for instance: 'If you circled A, we're in agreement that…' or : If you circled B, we're not in agreement that…' In this way, he indicates that there is no such thing as absolute truth. He tells us how he used *his* knowledge and experience to arrive at *his* conclusion.

Try it for yourself. Suppose a child does the sum 133 + 64 – 57 and arrives at the answer 130. Don't start by telling him it's wrong. Ask for instance: 'Gosh, I've got another answer. How did you get your answer?'

I would like to return to the little girl who lives next door that I mentioned in Chapter 3. To begin with, I kept hearing myself saying: 'Good girl!' I have now got myself used to saying: 'You did it!' or 'Yes!' when for instance with great difficulty, she gets her own shoes on or when she has been trying to throw stones into the water from a distance of two metres and finally succeeds. Of course, you might wonder what difference using those exact words would make; surely what's intended is more important? I use them because 'You did it!' better expresses what I want to say. When I say 'good girl', I give my approval. I decide that she is 'good' because she has done something that she couldn't do to begin with. With this, I indirectly imply that she must keep learning something all the time and that she should do her best. Because otherwise...

I can see and I know that she really doesn't need approval; that it would only get in her way. She puts her shoes on because she likes being able to. When she has achieved it, I'm happy for her. When I say 'you did it' or 'Yes!', I'm celebrating with her. When we're trying to throw stones in the water, we cheer when one lands in it. It makes no difference to her if the first six stones land on the grass. As far as she's concerned, she doesn't have to achieve anything.

I once translated an article of mine about wonderment into English. An English friend of mine offered to go through it with me to refine the English where necessary. We came across all sorts of words and phrases which he suggested changing. He got right into it, asked me questions. He really tried to select the words that came the closest to what I wanted to say. I really enjoyed working with him. He never once said that I'd got anything wrong. I have in the past translated several books from English into Dutch, and yet there I was, enjoying to the full this opportunity of brushing up my English. He wasn't telling me what I'd done wrong. He wanted to share his knowledge of English with me. He made suggestions. Sometimes, I didn't agree with him because he suggested something that didn't tally with what I wanted to say. We continued until both of us were completely satisfied with the text. We enjoyed ourselves so much that the time flew by. Before we knew it, two hours had gone by.

When we use the words 'good' and 'bad' we run the risk of getting involved in a discussion. If I say to someone who never buys organic food that organic food is good for his health, there is a good chance that he will contradict me. He will hear: 'Organic food is better than the rubbish you eat.' And who knows, that may be what I mean. I might also tell him how much I enjoy organic food. Then I am talking about myself. Why should I compare my eating habits with those of others? I have discovered that comparisons do not make me happier, and I'd rather be happy than right. In Dutch, there is only a small adjustment to be made to change the word for 'right' into the word for 'happiness': from 'gelijk' to 'geluk'.

Unfortunately, raising children has always relied heavily on making comparisons. In education, giving marks may well have been intended to give an objective indication of how much lesson material a child has at his command. I have always had my doubts about this, as I think marks are largely dependent on whether the questions happen to be about what the child has remembered of the lesson material. And with open questions, the marks are dependent on the judgment and interpretation of the teacher.

Within the family, comparisons are made between brothers and sisters, with children in the neighborhood, and with the children of friends. 'A child of four should be able to go to the toilet by himself. Our eldest could do it when he was four.' We also compare a child on one day with the same child on another day. 'She could wipe her own bottom yesterday. Why can't she do it now?'

I can think of all kinds of reasons why she may not be able to do it now. But that's not what I want to talk about here. What I want to say is that each person, and therefore each child is here and now, as he or she is. That's what I have to deal with, whether I like it or not. I can't change other people, even if I'd like to. So I try to accept what I see and hear as 'givens' without judgment. Deep within myself, I want to say 'yes' to every child and so encourage it to trust its own creativity and learning capabilities

I hope this chapter will inspire you to resolve to stop making comparisons and to look for alternatives. The exercises below are a start. Further suggestions follow in Chapter 11.

PRACTICE

- A number of situations are described below. Imagine you are involved in them. How would you respond without thinking or using the words good/right or bad/wrong/stupid? And without saying what would have been the better response.

1. Mary has got a 3 out of 10 for her geography test because she had learned Chapter 2 instead of Chapter 3.

2. Jenny has burned a hold in her sleeve while lighting the candles.

3. Tim has brushed his teeth without you even having to ask him to.

4. You come home with a bag full of shopping and your son offers to make you a cup of tea.

5. Patrick hasn't hung his coat up and it is now lying on the floor in the living room.

- Think of an object you are happy to have around. Something you own or something you use regularly. Take the time to think about how happy you are with it.

Then compare it with similar, but more beautiful, better or more useful objects. How does this affect how you feel about it?

- About which of your qualities are you completely content? Sit down quietly and enjoy how useful it is that you have this quality or everything you have achieved as a result. You can write it down if this helps you.

Now compare yourself with other people who also have this quality, but have achieved more with it. Perhaps they have even become famous as a result. Perhaps you know someone who is just as outspoken as you are, but has more tact, so doesn't so readily get involved in arguments. If you muse on this for a little, you will notice that the contentment you felt to begin with will change into discontent.

7

DEMOCRATIC DISCIPLINE

A reaction I often get to my unusual angle on rewards is: 'Giving rewards may be a kind of punishment and have all sorts of disadvantages, but if I stop doing it, there'll be trouble. Chidren don't know about discipline. It's my job as an adult to make sure they do.'

I understand this concern. If we're used to being the authority and to exerting discipline from this position, ceasing to give rewards would mean giving up that role and having nothing to replace it with. We might lose control over the situation, a prospect which may cause us anxiety. Perhaps we already do relax the reins sometimes, but the result is always immediate chaos. With this in mind, we resolve time and time again to be even stricter. But this too is hard to maintain, with the result that the children again start to slip through our fingers from time to time. It's very much like being on a train traveling between two stations: the station of authoritarian discipline and the station of giving in. This comparison was made by Aletha Solter, an American developmental psychologist. It appears that there is no choice other than to travel back and forth endlessly between these two stations. But wait – that's strange! Halfway along the tracks is another station. We hadn't noticed it before. We can alight from the train here and go for a walk in the Woods of Democratic Discipline. Solter uses the word 'democratic' in the sense of 'with input from all those involved'. In these woods, we come across all sorts of things like responsibility, interdependence, creativity, acceptance and respect, cooperation, problem-solving skills, self-discipline, self-worth, kindly interestedness. I'm suggesting that we pack these skills and qualities away into our mental knapsacks and when we get home, lay them out on the table with the intention of getting to know this wealth better.

Dennis's teacher has decided to create more space for children's own sense of responsibility. Dennis, aged five, has his moments of being rowdy when he doesn't feel like cooperating: after the gym lesson for instance. The other children are getting dressed, but Dennis is running around in his gym shorts and is screaming that he's going to smash this and that. His teacher knows he is capable of dressing himself and she already has her hands full helping children who aren't.

In the past, she would have given Dennis a stern talking to, or promised him that he could walk next to her on the way back to the classroom if he got dressed immediately (authoritarian discipline). If this hadn't worked, the teacher would have helped him to dress in the end (giving in). She would have done this with abrupt movements, positively bristling with reproach.

Now, she just asks if he would please like to get his clothes on. She accepts and respects his rowdiness. She shows kindly interest in how he is now and doesn't laugh at him in front of his classmates. When everyone is nearly ready, she says: 'I don't want you to get left behind here. Come along in your shorts and T-shirt.' By doing this, she still takes responsibility for Dennis's safety.

Dennis can now choose for himself how he wants to go back to the classroom. His sense of self-worth is safe now. Within two minutes, he has finished dressing. He has taken responsibility for how he is dressed for the walk back to the classroom: in his gym clothes or in his school clothes. If this situation is repeated often, Dennis may at some point learn the self-discipline needed to get himself ready on time. This discipline will not have been imposed on him by the teacher.

I have found out for myself that there's a world of difference between forcing others to do what I want them to do (or be what I want them to be), and being clear about what my values and wishes are and then placing them alongside those of other people. I see how people blossom when I do this. They feel they have space in which to grow. They have free choice as to whether they follow my example or advice or do things another way. And I see the kind of self-discipline that develops from this.

My daughter, for instance, has a different style of getting things finished 'on time' or of arriving 'on time' than I do. I worried about it for years. I tried to teach her to be on time by telling her, around ten minutes before she had to leave, everything she still had to do before she could get out of the door. Or by reminding her to do her homework at moments when she was having a nice chat with her sister. I tried to teach her my way, my discipline. *I* prefer to have things ready an hour or a day in advance. Only then do *I* have the peace of mind to read or go for a bike-ride.

A couple of years ago, I let go of trying to force my sort of discipline on my daughter. (In any case, my efforts had not had the desired effect. They just put me in a ratty mood, full of reproach.) In the beginning, I would now and then slip back into my old patterns, but more and more, I kept my attention on how she dealt with time. I admired the calm and good-humor with which she packed her things, listened to me and had something to tell me, right up until the moment she needed to leave for school. I have seen how she sat at the table with her maths and alternated doing sums with making telephone calls, drawing, chatting and reading a magazine. And how she proudly came home with excellent marks.

More recently, I get the impression that she can work on something continuously for a longer period than she used to be able to. Could it be that she now has more peace and flexibility in which to do things her own way and is therefore able to concentrate for longer? After all, we all want to get the most out of life!

I am convinced that no one chooses to make chaos out of their lives or to forever postpone dealing with problems. Sometimes we dread doing something and prefer not to think about it. Other people don't help by continually nagging about when we're finally going to get around to it. It may be helpful if someone sees that we're having difficulties and listens to us. Having a good moan or telling someone how difficult something is for us can be enough to get us going again. Sometimes more is needed before we feel able to deal with our responsibilities. Just think about all those people who leave school early and then later, when they're twenty or thirty, follow evening courses to get the knowledge they need to get along in their chosen field of work.

I was once supervising a girl of seventeen while she was doing a project of several months' duration. Three weeks before she was supposed to make a presentation, she had almost nothing on paper. She later told me that the way I had dealt with this was what had saved her. I paid attention to her feelings, her struggle, I looked into the subject matter of the project and made the occasional suggestion. If she rejected it, I asked her why she did so. I didn't reproach her, made no demands and didn't take over her responsibility for getting the project finished in time. She told me that she had been reproaching herself so much and had been making such high demands of herself that she was more or less paralyzed. By watching the example I set her, she was able to stop doing this, and find the self-discipline to get the job done.

Self-discipline comes from a combination of freedom and order, according to Krishnamurti. Freedom doesn't mean 'doing whatever you want', because people cannot live independently of others. If we do what we want without reference to what other people might want, those other people's freedom will be infringed and this can throw things into disarray, as for instance, when one child runs through the classroom screaming, while the others are trying to listen to a story.

The freedom I'm talking about is an inner freedom from greed, from wanting to be the best, and from cruelty. We can demonstrate this 'self-discipline in freedom' and give children the opportunity of developing their own discipline. Your help, in the sense of being there alongside them as they discover their own unique way of achieving this, will definitely be appreciated.

Being disciplined is easier for some people than for others. It depends on their ability to postpone pleasure: first doing something they don't enjoy and only then doing what they do enjoy. Children sometimes find this very difficult. They want to play with the building blocks *now*, not clear up the crayons first. A teenager will want to go to the cinema *now* and not do his homework first.

Whether or not we are able to postpone having fun has to do with how motivated we are. Give a child the chance to find out if clearing up his toys has advantages. He will notice he can find everything easily. Things don't get so easily lost, things don't break so quickly. There's more room on the table to play with something else. He will notice that his mother seems to like it when the room stays tidy. These advantages may stimulate an inner motivation to first put away the crayons before playing with the building blocks. This may take a number of years, by the way, so it may be more a question of clearing up school-books by the time he does it.

I notice that clearing up is a daily source of irritation for many parents and teachers. This was also true when my children were small. When I was a child myself, my mother got irritated at the mess made by me and my brothers and sisters. When I talk to parents about it now, I hear: 'The person who takes something out of the cupboard must be the one to put it back'; 'Well, they'll need to keep their own houses tidy when they grow up'; 'You've got to train them when they're young'; 'I'm not a slave'; 'I just hate mess'.

What a lot of basic needs (see Chapter 3) there are at the bottom of these remarks! We want children to make a contribution; we worry about when they're grown up; we like to be treated with respect; we enjoy peace and quiet; and, we think a tidy room is more attractive.

Perhaps we would be happy for the children to make a different sort of contribution from what we first had in mind? Or perhaps they're already doing so? Can we trust that the children will develop their own way of dealing with chaos? Do we tidy up the children's things because they tell us to or because we want to? Can we set an example and show that we not only enjoy a tidy room, but the tidying too?

If tidying up is fun, we get started on it sooner, of course. Children of two or thereabouts often still enjoy it. But once parents discover that their kids can put the building blocks in the box themselves and start exerting pressure, the fun expires in no time. If you have to do something, it can't possibly be nice. In many families, there is already a power-struggle before the children are three. This is a shame, as it doesn't have to be like this.

It may of course be that a child sees only disadvantages in tidying up. It takes time and having all that stuff around you is quite fun. If we stop doling out rewards and punishments, what occurs may very well be quite different from what we had originally intended. This takes some getting used to.

It might for instance be that together, parents and children decide that tidying up just once a day or once a week suits them best. Or that they both enjoy it best if the one who is troubled by the mess tidies it up. If we agree that they need only tidy their own rooms when they want to themselves, or can see the point, it may happen only three times a year.

Can we, as parents, summon the patience to wait until our children have the inner motivation to take our wishes into account and to tidy up? Or to do it from an inner desire?

Employing extrinsic motivation, by giving a child a reward if he tidies up for instance, may seem to be a quicker method. But we run the risk of the child developing an energetic dislike for tidying up. And a sense of being wronged for all those times he didn't tidy up and didn't get the reward. There is even the chance that for the rest of his life, cleaning will become something he tries to postpone. Or he may develop the habit of always tidying everything up immediately without pleasure, because he would feel guilty if he didn't. The pressure is then no longer coming from the outside world, but from within.

So by exercising patience, and by making agreements in an atmosphere of humor and flexibility (after discussing the pros and cons of either option for both parties), we can give our children the chance to develop self-discipline. Whatever agreements we make, we shouldn't be satisfied until everyone is happy with them. We can keep our children involved in the discussions by asking them for their ideas and suggestions.

And in the meantime, we can choose to tidy up our children's things ourselves every now and then. Not from a position of: 'I'm fed up with this mess!', but because we'd like to, because we want to set an example, because we want peace and harmony, and a tidy house would help.

I once talked to a mother who had for years tried to get her three sons to put their shoes in the shoe cupboard instead of leaving them lying in front of the sofa where they had kicked them off. She kept demanding that they tidy their shoes away. When I asked her whether this had the desired effect, she said with some degree of surprise: 'No, it doesn't.' During the conversation which followed, it turned out that when the boys didn't put their shoes away, she had all kinds of thoughts: 'I'm just the skivvy round here. They have no idea what I do for them. And then they don't even tidy up their own shoes. Outrageous!' I asked if she received other kinds of acknowledgement for her care or whether the boys let her know that they loved her. Oh, that wasn't a problem. She was then able to see the shoe problem for what it was. For the boys, sinking back onto the sofa and taking their shoes off meant peace at last. For her, the shoes in the shoe-cupboard meant a calm, pleasant room. From that moment on, the shoes no longer presented a problem. She tidied the shoes up herself or she waited for a moment when one of the boys got up from the sofa to ask him to put his shoes away. Once the tense, argumentative atmosphere around this question had disappeared, she spoke to her sons about it again. The youngest, aged seven, then made a suggestion: 'I'd be perfectly happy to take my shoes off before I sit on the sofa. Mum, will your remind me if I forget?' And whether she wanted to or not, well, that could be another topic for discussion.

Some parents and teachers are afraid that their children or pupils will learn nothing at school – for instance, that they will never learn basic arithmetic – if the adults do not keep discipline. If we search with our children for what it is they want to find out and what means suits them the best, we provide space for them. Learning is then such fun that we can hardly even speak of discipline.

There are schools where children can choose for themselves what they will learn and when they will learn it. In practice, it would seem that once they have found a purpose for learning arithmetic, they do this with a drive that no learning programme from the external world can compete with. This purpose may be anything: playing a game with two dice, handling money, building a house in the garden or becoming an architect.

PRACTICE

-Take some time to think about the following questions. What is your stance on tidying up? Do you insist on it? How was tidying up dealt with at home when you were a child? Can you see a link between how you were brought up and how you now deal with clearing up? Is there something you'd like to change in this area? How can you motivate yourself to do it?

There are various ways in which you can change. You may want to tidy up more, or more frequently, or you might want to loosen up a bit, even if other people have left things lying around. Or maybe there's something else you'd like to change. And perhaps you don't want to change anything.

-Pay attention to whether there are moments when you behave as an authority figure. This may be towards a child or towards an adult.

I will give two examples. You can replace these with your own examples.

-Dirty washing is constantly left lying around all over the house and you want to decide how to solve the problem. You know you have right on your side and, using manipulation, you try to exert your right. You punish recalcitrance by getting angry, and willingness to please is rewarded with praise. 'You're showing some sense at last, good girl.'

-A couple of children in your class are continually creating a disturbance. You demand quiet. When this doesn't help, you promise to read to the class for ten minutes extra if they're quiet for the rest of the lesson.

Later, when you're alone, think about how you might have dealt with these situations in another way. Alight from the Train of Control, walk through the Woods of Alternative Possibilities. What do you come across?

Write about it in a journal if you want to.

Imagine yourself getting down off your throne and sitting opposite the other person or people in the scenario. Ask about the other people's viewpoint, and what they would like. Tell them how you see things. Enjoy the differences in vision and solutions. Look at everyone's underlying needs.

Can you arrive at an agreement by which both parties take responsibility for whatever is in question, be it the dirty washing or quiet in the classroom? In other words, can you both summon self-discipline, because you both want not only your own needs, but also those of the other to be met?

8

REASONS FOR DOING WHAT'S ASKED

When we reward children, we get them to do what we want. The reason they do this is either that they like rewards or that they enjoy being praised. In either case, they become dependent on our stickers, money or approval to feel good about themselves. They may for instance, feel proud of a drawing if they see that we like it, and find fault with it if we don't. In the end, the motivation to draw at all may only come from the outside world.

Is this what we want? No, we gave our rewards because we thought our children would be happy with them, or that we were helping them to fit into the world around them. But in actual fact, we didn't do it only for the children. We felt good about ourselves as we did it. It gave us something to hold onto. The children did what we wanted, and harmony prevailed.

I use the past tense here, but we may not yet be willing to say goodbye to our trusty rewards system because we're vary partial to it. And it works, doesn't it? In any case, the kids do as we ask and are happy with their reward or our words of praise. What do you think? Do rewards also lead to insight and voluntary cooperation?

I'll give another example. Suppose our son of seven doesn't cope well with his days if he isn't in bed by seven o'clock. We've tried everything: being patient, getting angry, coercion. We have also discovered that he goes up to bed with no problem if he knows that he'll get a five-minute foot-massage if he's in bed by five to seven. Phew! Peace at last! The argument looks watertight. Contented parents, contented child and he's in bed on time. Now I'm going to throw a couple of spanners in the works. He has to earn the foot massage and he doesn't get it if he isn't in bed in time. If we notice that the massage helps to calm him down and go to sleep more easily, why make it conditional? I suspect that both parties would enjoy the massage more and that our son would get more out of it if it was given purely out of loving care.

That's one spanner. The second is that I'm concerned that this solution will only work temporarily. One day, he will have had enough of massages. Or he'll want us to sing him a song with it. And read him a story too. At a certain point, we'll be sitting there with a long face, working our way through a nightly ritual. Or we may imagine after a couple of weeks, that the massage should no longer be necessary to get him to fall asleep. Would our son still meekly go upstairs at half past six? He still hasn't understood that he'll feel better next day if he gets a good night's sleep.

And now we arrive at the question: what do I want a child's reason to be for doing as I say? I will first say what I *don't* want his reason to be. I don't want him to do it just because I say so. I don't want to be the authority that makes decisions for others. At the moment when *I* decide that seven o'clock is the best bedtime for a child, I lose contact with the little person with all his continually changing feelings and needs. I don't want to manipulate. This doesn't mean that we must always allow children to have their own way. In our new world without manipulation, I don't think the aim is for everyone just to do what he feels like the whole time. This would mean chaos and may bring danger and sorrow with it. I think it would be useful for us to learn to take each other's wishes into account without having to be forced to do so.

I like it when children find other people's wishes just as important as their own; when they follow their own hearts as they explore and play and are at their happiest when everyone is happy: a sort of 'us feeling'. I am reminded of the African concept of Ubuntu, which means something like 'I'm happy if you are'. In Africa, they want to breathe new life into this concept, at teacher-training colleges amongst other places, so students can pass it on to their pupils at a later date. But there is interest in Ubuntu in Europe as well.

As a parent or teacher, we can help children to take others into account by putting into words what we see them do so that they can become aware of it. If Peter knocks over another child's house of building blocks with his tricycle, we might say: 'Oh, now the house has fallen down. Mary is upset. Would you ride over there, please?' And we can turn the nose of the tricycle in the other direction. If Peter comes back to demolish the house again and again, he is indicating that he enjoys the effect of the falling blocks. He doesn't know how to achieve this effect without upsetting Mary. You can help him by providing him with his own set of building blocks. He can then build as high as he likes and knock them over to his heart's content. So we don't make the assumption that Peter's intention is to upset Mary.

You may be thinking 'All well and good, but what use is all this to me in daily life.' If I'm about to go out shopping with my daughter, and I ask her to get her coat on ready to go, it's nice if she does it. If I stand in front of the class and ask the children to tidy away their exercise books and come to the gym hall with me, the sense of peace in school will benefit if they obey promptly. So I do sometimes want children to do as I say.

I think that children's well-being is better served if their reasons for doing as we tell them are as follows:

-because they want to, and not because they have to;

-because they enjoy doing something for another person, they want to take others into account;

- because they enjoy doing things together;

- because they choose for harmony or peace; sometimes it's just nice to do what someone says, then you don't have to think for yourself;

- because they are hungry for learning and new experiences;

- because they respect the agreement that you as a parent (and certainly as a teacher) sometimes have the role of organiser. (This respect can only occur when the adult has shown that he or she has respect for who the child is and what's going on inside him or her);

- because they trust that the adults have their best interests at heart, and that in some situations, they have an overview of what's the best thing to do.

In the points above, I am looking entirely from the child's point of view. We have looked at the reasons a child has for doing as we say. We can turn this question around. *What do I want my reasons to be for asking a child to do as I say?* These might be my reasons:

- At a given moment, I think I know what the child needs. I take responsibility for meeting such needs as safety and rest. I want to protect the child against calamity (see also p. 36 on protective force). In this last case, I may use coercion.

- Otherwise, I would only want a child to obey me if he does so voluntarily, for the reasons named above.

-With a group of children, it is sometimes useful if one person makes the decisions. As the teacher is the leader and has an overview, it is logical for him or her to make these decisions. In this case, the reason is to ensure a pleasant working environment.

- There are limits to my energy and I have my needs too. Sometimes I want a child to do as I say because that would meet my need for rest and pleasure. If this is the reason, I could use coercion, but that's not what I want. I want to be clear about my request. I can insist by repeating my request, or by backing it up with arguments. But I remain conscious of the fact that there are always other ways of meeting these needs of mine for rest or pleasure. Meeting my needs can never depend on one specific action from one specific child. I simply don't believe this.

An example to clarify this last point:

Maggie and Ginette are squabbling. They both want to sit on the same chair. Martin, their father, has just got home from work. He is tired and just wants to collapse on the sofa and listen to some music quietly. After five minutes, he asks the children if they'd like to stop arguing and try to work out a solution to their problem. This strikes me as a clear request. The wrangling continues for a couple of minutes. Martin now insists by telling them how he is feeling and what he wants. He adds: 'I'm not in the mood for this racket.' It doesn't work. The children are probably also tired and this is their way of dealing with it. Martin will have to think of another approach if he wants his needs met. He can shift to another room, he can use the headphones and ignore the squabbling, he can give his kids a couple of dollars to buy ice-cream, he can change tack and go and have a romp with them and so on. He can of course also shout at them and make both children sit on a different chair. I would however, question whether that would get him the rest he longs for.

The emphasis of this book is on children's well-being. We may occasionally think: 'And what about me? I have my needs too.' I am well aware of this. And I am convinced that caring for and raising children becomes a considerably lighter task if parents/teachers know what they need and take care of getting it. So if we're tired, let's make sure the kids play at their friends' houses more often, or be a little less strict about getting through all the lesson material at school. Everyone will be better off for it.

How do we indicate where our limits are? Do we know when we've reached our limits and if so, do we mention it? Would we rather something doesn't happen, but not mind too much if it does anyway? What do we really want done our way, and what do we definitely not want? What decisions are we genuinely happy to leave to the child?

While I was bringing up my own children, I noticed that they benefited from clarity. When I really meant something, they would comply with my wishes without a murmur. For instance, it was important to me to have a few hours for myself in the evenings. During the day, I was fully available to my kids, but that was easier for me if I was able to devote myself entirely to my own things in the evening. Apparently, I radiated this so clearly in my whole attitude, voice and words that my children only ever got out of bed in exceptional circumstances. When I had trouble identifying my standpoint and wasn't clear about what I wanted, they could whinge for hours. I remember once when my daughter wanted a friend to stay overnight on a weekday. She took me by surprise with her request, and I hesitated. Even when I had said 'no', she returned to the subject several times that afternoon. I also sometimes said 'no' to things when it really didn't make much difference to me whether they happened or not. I would then spend a lot of energy and attention on preventing it from happening. I now realize that it would have been more useful if I had been more selective about when I said 'no' and allowed my children to mess about a bit more.

I got a second chance while minding the little girl from next door aged three. Some time ago, she was playing with her Duplo. She built a house and put her toy animals inside it. When she had had enough of this, she smashed the whole thing with wild movements and marched with sturdy steps through the wreckage, sending everything flying in all directions. I let her be. Possibly she was frustrated because nothing had worked out as she had wanted. Or she had a preference for physical exuberance over quiet, concentrated play. When, a little later, she started to throw the bricks around the room, I intervened. I took her hand, and said clearly: 'No, I don't want you to do that! I'm afraid something will break or I'll get hit on the head by one of the bricks. That would hurt.' I was selective about when I expressed my limits, so there weren't as many for her to deal with, making the situation simpler to understand. I suspect that children will tend to keep within our boundaries more often if there aren't too many of them.

PRACTICE

-What are your reasons for rewarding the people in your life? Think of concrete situations when you rewarded someone either with something tangible or with your words. What did you want to achieve? Did it have the desired effect? You can write about this or talk to someone about it.

-What would you like the reasons to be for a child (or an adult) to do what you ask? Think of several concrete situations. These may be events in the past, but they may also concern things you're planning to ask of people.

-What would you like your reasons to be for asking a child (or an adult) to do as you say? Again, this may be based on events from the past or in the future. You may also like to think up a hypothetical case, but preferably one which could happen.

-Describe a situation in which you went so far beyond your limits that you ended up furious or exhausted or perhaps even ill or totally overstrung. Look for the moment at which your limit was reached. If this had been clear to you then, what might you have done or said to prevent the unhappy results?

Realizing how stupid you were is not the issue here. We are confronted with situations like these because they contain lessons for life, so seize the opportunity and don't let those learning moments pass by unused.

9

HEARING THE 'YES' IN A CHILD'S 'NO'

No always means yes to something else. So no is not the end, but the beginning of a conversation.
Inbal Kashtan

The answer to the question 'What would I like the reason to be for a child to do as I ask?' could be summarized thus: I'd like the child to say 'yes' to my request voluntarily. But what do we do when a child doesn't say 'yes', but 'no'?

If a child says no, we can respond in a variety of ways. We can accept no for an answer and comply with the child's wishes. Our request was after all a request and not a demand. Here is an example of saying okay to a no.

A nurse asks: 'Peter, would you get out of bed and sit on the chair for a moment?' Peter looks sullen and says; 'No, I want to stay in bed.' The nurse sees that the sheets still look reasonably clean and says: 'Shall we do it tomorrow?' Peter gives a small nod of the head and shuts his eyes.

The nurse acknowledges and respects Peter's desire for rest. The result will be very different from the results we would get if we were to react to every no from a child with: 'No? Well see if I care.' Or: 'All right, I'll do it myself then.' In this way, we would give the child the opportunity to become a little tyrant.

By now you will have understood that I am not an advocate of forcing a child to do something it doesn't want to do nor of taking the indirect route of punishing or rewarding. But how *can* we react then?

Raising children is usually okay until a child says 'no'. Help! What now? I am reminded of a letter written to Inbal Kashtan, Nonviolent Communication trainer and writer and quoted in her book 'Parenting from your Heart'.

It's about Shelly and her husband who have a daughter Grace, aged three. Grace sometimes refuses to sit in the children's car seat. They pick her up bodily and lift her in. They do this to protect their child from danger. They could of course also wait and only drive off when they have verbally persuaded her to climb in on her own accord. But, like most people, they are often in a hurry. So waiting isn't an option. What can they do about this?

Let's assume that Shelly and her husband are looking for solutions that will appeal to both their daughter and themselves. The key to finding a point of contact when hearing a no, is remembering that 'no' always means 'yes' to something else. So it indicates not the end, but the beginning of a conversation. If parents first take the time to make contact, similar conversations may take less time than the method of first asking politely, then insisting and finally coercing. In the phase of trying out new things like this, I would certainly recommend trying to respond in the manner described below first in an unhurried situation when we're not under pressure to get something done *now*. When we have gained more proficiency at this sort of conversation, we can use these techniques under more hectic conditions.

Inbal Kashtan gives us the following example:

Shelly: Hey it's time to leave to go to Grandpa's.

Grace: NO! NO! NO!

Shelly: Are you enjoying what you'r'e doing and want

to continue doing it? *(Instead of hearing the "no,", Shelly listens for what Grace is saying "yes" to by guessing her feeling of pleasure and her needs for play and choice.)*

> *Grace*: YES! I want to keep gardening!
> *Shelly*: You're really having fun gardening?
> *Grace*: Yes!
> *Shelly*: I'm enjoying seeing how fun it is for you. I'm worried because I like getting to places when I say I will. *(Instead of coming back with her own "no," Shelly expresses her feelings and her need for responsibility.)* If we want to get to Grandpa's when I told him we'll be there, this is the time to leave. So would you be willing to get into the car seat now? *(Shelly ends with a request that lets Grace know what she can do to help Shelly meet her needs.)*
> *Grace*: NO! I want to garden now.
> *Shelly*: I'm confused about what to do. I like it when you do things you enjoy, and I also want to do what I said I was going to do. *(Shelly shows Grace that she cares about meeting both their needs.)* Would you be willing to go into the car seat in 5 minutes so we could get there soon? *(Shelly offers a strategy that might meet both their needs, again in the form of a request.)*

As Kashtan says, it may not go this easily. Grace may continue to say 'no'. Her desire for autonomy may be so strong that she will be prepared to cooperate only if she is given the opportunity to help think of ways in which both Mum and she can be satisfied. We may be surprised at how creative children of even two or three can be in thinking up solutions. Who knows, maybe Grace will arrive at the idea of picking a couple of flowers from her garden to take to Grandpa or of taking her rake and spade so she can do some gardening at Grandpa's.

Shelly can also think up some creative ideas. She could

ring Grandpa, for instance and discuss how it would be for him if they come this afternoon instead of this morning. If Shelly has reached her limit and decides to leave for Grandpa's now, she can still stay in contact with Grace by verbalizing what she guesses is going on in Grace. While she picks her up calmly, she might say: 'You're really upset you can't go on playing in your garden, hey? I wish you could too. I really want to go to Grandpa's now, so I'm taking you with me in the car.' No grumbling, no comforting words like: 'You can play some more when we're back. I'm sure there's something you'd like to play with at Grandpa's.' This may be true, but Grace probably isn't interested at the moment. What she needs is acknowledgement of her disappointment, sorrow and/or anger.

Some children may stubbornly persist in saying 'no' because they have to do what other people say too often for their taste. Their need for autonomy gets stronger and stronger and screams out for fulfillment. If they often experience adults taking their needs into account, taking their wishes seriously, they will be less inclined to dig in their heels. They will learn to trust adults' intentions. They will discover that people do listen to them when they say 'no'. They will no longer need to fight for attention and respect, because they already have it. There will then be space for another need: contributing to others' pleasure.

PRACTICE

Think of a number of examples of situations in which a child has said 'no' to a request of yours. Think (and write down if you like) how you might respond to the child in the spirit of this chapter. You can create a dialogue of it like the one between Shelly and Grace. You could also do a role-play: you play the child and someone else plays you. This gives you the opportunity of empathizing with the child's position.

- Below are a number of children's no-sentences. What might the child say yes to?

1. No, I don't want to help her with her sums.

2. No, I don't want to do the washing-up.

3. No, I won't go to bed.

4. No, she can't play with my doll.

5. No, I won't eat my sandwich.

10

TAKING CARE OF OURSELVES FIRST

It is of vital importance to me that a child learns to take his own wishes seriously. This becomes easier if we set an example and take our own wishes seriously. When I was small, I learned always to put others first. It was selfish and therefore bad to think of myself first. I gradually discovered that I am only able to help others whole-heartedly and with all my energy if I have taken care of myself first. I have now found a balance. I love doing things for others when I have made sure that I've had sufficient relaxation and solitude.

Okay, my children have left home, so it's easy for me to talk. It's different if you've got two little ones rushing around you all day long, or perhaps even a whole class full. Then you don't have time to even think that you might need something occasionally. It isn't easy. But I do believe it's possible.

I have sometimes observed parents and teachers when I was on the look-out for people who appear relatively untroubled by tiredness or irritation. I found a striking example in a friend of mine. He is a sculptor. He and his wife have four children between the ages of three and ten. His wife is often ill and is then unable to do much with the children. They don't have a lot of money. They have just moved house and he has built a couple of small rooms in the attic. On top of all this, his left arm has been paralyzed since he was seventeen as the result of an accident. He can only use the arm for supporting things.

When I had just got to know him, I was surprised that he always arrived at school with his children on time. He always seemed to be calm. I have never seen him look rushed or agitated. He also always has time for a chat. I was visiting his home once, the evening before his eldest son's birthday. He was busy until half past twelve, hanging streamers, baking a cake, packing presents. While I was helping him, we talked and talked. We had lots of fun and we didn't get tired, so time wasn't an issue.

I asked him how he stuck at this task, which to me looked heavy, without getting ill or overwrought. He told me it wasn't a question of sticking at anything. He really enjoys his life and that's because of the choices he makes. He consciously chose to take on the responsibility of bringing up his four children. He doesn't spend his time thinking about everything he used to be able to do in the past. He doesn't worry about the future. He lives in the here and now, so his head is free for the organizing and caring that goes with running a household for six people. He does this so efficiently that he has an hour for himself almost every day in which to read or work on a sculpture. On days when this isn't so, he gets his energy from a conversation carried on at the edge of the swimming pool during a swimming lesson or from the creativity invested in producing a meal. He is closely involved in the ins and outs of the children's lives, is always there for them if they're having a tough time, afraid or needing his help. He sets his boundaries clearly. I sometimes get the impression that the children do what he suggests so readily because he is a child with them, while at the same time, taking the lead. They trust that what he suggests will be either fun or useful.

In this man, I found an example of someone who can wholly be there for his children because he takes such good care of himself.

I'm not saying that this is *the* way for everyone to take care of him or herself. Comparing ourselves with others just makes us unhappy.

I'll name a variety of ways we might use on the path to taking care of ourselves. Raising children means to some degree, setting an example. If we take our own wishes seriously, we stimulate our children to do the same. So if the loaded word 'egotism' looms up again, we can remind ourselves that we're not only doing it for ourselves, but that our children will also benefit. Taking the advice of a therapist, I once hung the following motto on my mirror: 'If I take care of myself, that's the example my children will see'. It's been hanging there for years.

- Enjoy a hot bath, an hour's shopping or reading. Make space for it in your diary. Don't think: 'I'll do that when I've got some spare time.' I can assure you that there's no such thing as spare time. Do this, if you can, without feeling guilty. Without fail, a child will sense it if you are feeling guilty, whether you express it in words or not.

- Say 'no' clearly if you don't want something. Have compassion for the difficulty your child has with your 'no', but remain clear. 'No, you're not having a biscuit now. I can see you'd really like one. That's tough for you. The answer is still no.' Even if children then begin to whine, there is nothing more you need to say. 'No' is 'no'. The clearer you are, the sooner they will give up whining. They'll notice it doesn't help anyway.

- Be clear about what you need and when you're not feeling well. When I was a child, I thought my mother was never weak or ill. She was always even-tempered, caring and interested. I sometimes wondered if she felt anything. She was angry sometimes, but I thought that was because of us. We had obviously done something wrong. I later understood that she was angry at times when she could no longer suppress her discontent. Children are generally eager to take care of you if you're not well.

- Ask children to help you or do something for you if you're having a difficult time. Say to the class, for instance, at the beginning of the handicrafts lesson: 'I'm not feeling very well. Would you all help me as much as possible? Then I can stay sitting down. Of course if you can't work something out amongst yourselves, you can come to me.'

- Accept help offered by other adults with open arms. If no -one offers any help, ask for it. Be careful about who you ask what and whether you think the person will have time and space to help you. When my children were of junior school age, there was a period in which I was very ill. I was often told that people really liked the way I allowed myself to be helped without embarrassment and asked for help if it didn't happen of its own accord. Think about it - if someone you know is having a difficult time, you feel sympathy and you want to do something. If someone is clear about what they would like you to do, you feel relieved.

- In hard times, give yourself the advice you would give your friends in a similar situation. 'Just let things be for today.' 'Don't worry so much.' 'Don't be so serious. Laughter's the best medicine.' If someone else says something like this to you, it often may not help. But who knows - it may just help if you say it yourself.

- Make sure you eat healthily and drink enough. When my children were small, I seemed to spend the whole day making and serving fruit snacks, biscuits and cups of milk. It didn't occur to me that I could get myself something to drink between meals too. There was a time when I never made tea or coffee for myself, ate no fruit and at mealtimes, fed myself only the occasional mouthful of food in between feeding the children. Nowadays, I drink at least two litres of water alone. I wish I had done that then too.

PRACTICE

- Think of a time when you weren't enjoying yourself. This could be any situation. Someone might have been telling you a story and you didn't feel like listening. Or you were in someone else's house and feeling cold or wanting a sandwich. Or you slept badly the night before you had to give eight hours' worth of lessons. What did you do to start enjoying yourself again? Or didn't you do anything? What would you like to have done?

- What are the ways *you* take care of yourself? Perhaps some of them are mentioned in this chapter. Are there others? Pick one way that works well for you. Write about it. Tell someone else about your ways, how you use them. Give examples. By doing this, you will become more aware of your methods. This may help you to use them more often and at moments when you might otherwise not have thought of them.

- You could choose to write or talk about a way of taking care of yourself that you would like to adopt. Look amongst the people you know and see if there is anyone who uses this way of taking care of themselves with ease. See what tricks they use and add them to your own box of tricks.

11

LIST OF ALTERNATIVES TO REWARDS

AND PUNISHMENT

In the previous chapters, you have read about quite a few alternatives to rewards and punishment. In this chapter, I have ordered them in a conveniently arranged list for easy reference.

- *Enjoying things together.* When a child has got all his sums right or has tidied up his room, he'll be feeling proud or pleased with himself. This pleasure is magnified if someone enjoys it with him. We can put the child's feelings into words by saying how wonderful it is for him that he can do this sort of sum now or by asking him what he found while he was tidying up his room or why he likes his room to be tidy. While doing this, we can show that when he's happy, we're happy too. This is different from showing that we are happy because he's done something so well. That would be giving praise. It may actually be possible for us to be happy with what we consider to be a mess, because we enjoy the fact that the child has chosen to do what makes him happy. From what he has said, it is clear that *he* wants to decide how his room will look and to have his things close to him within easy reach if he chooses. If everything is in a cupboard or a drawer, he can't see it, he has to look for it.

- *Lamenting together.* A child who has had an argument with a friend will be even more upset if we respond with: 'When are you going to learn to take what she wants into account!' We can say what we think the child is feeling and lament with her. 'Are you feeling sad because you both wanted to do something different?' Parents so much want their children to be happy that they often tend to try to comfort them: 'Here's a kiss. All better now,' or to distract them. I notice that children and other people like it if I'm just there for them in silence, sometimes with an arm around the shoulders so they're not alone with their pain or sorrow. Sorrow, just as any other emotion, is neither good nor bad. It just *is*....full stop.

- *Express our gratitude.* When a child has done something you are happy with, say it. Say: 'Thank you for tidying up the kitchen', 'Thank you for telling me about your day. Now I know how you are.' Expressing gratitude can grow into a habit. It helps us focus on the things that enrich life and seems a warm and joyful alternative for 'You are so good!'

Once I started a workshop with asking the participants to share their gratitude towards themselves and others. It gave us so much joy that we continued doing this for two hours.

I suggest you find your own time and place to pay attention to gratitude: during a shared meal, at bed time, at the end of a school-day or -week, at a scheduled time during school-meetings amongst colleagues.

- *Say how we feel about things.* Say what we feel and what we would like when a child is throwing stones at another child. We might for instance say that we're worried because we don't want anyone to get hurt (if possible, holding the arm of the child throwing stones so he can't throw any more.) We can say what we would like, beginning our message with the word 'I'. And when a child is happily drawing, we might say we're happy to see him enjoying his work. However, if the child is deeply involved in his drawing, we should keep silent. Children at play can become totally absorbed in their own world, experiencing what we adults might call religion or spirituality. It would sometimes be a great pity to interrupt this intimacy.

- *Focus attention on the effect of what a child says or does.* I see adults do this when children do something which is unpleasant for another child or person. 'Look at Yolanda's face. I think she looks sad. Why do you think that is?' We could also do this when a child has given away half of her biscuit. 'Look at Nina's big smile. I think she's really happy with her piece of biscuit.'

- *Show interest.* We can do this regardless of whether something is 'good' or 'bad'. We can show genuine interest in what motivated a child to do something the way he did. Whether he has written 'he doesn't' or 'he don't', we can ask what made him write it and ask if he would like to hear what the rule was again.

We can also show interest after the event. A child concentrating on a game will sometimes prefer to play on. He may enjoy the occasional pat on the head or our coming to sit down beside him and joining in. A child who is bored and is interfering with other children may need a bit more time to feel comfortable before she goes and plays herself. It may be that something is bothering her and she might like us to take her aside and chat to her. We are then showing interest in her as a person, without judging her

- *Be clear.* One of the reasons we give rewards is that we want to make it clear to children how we expect them to behave and what they need to know to be able to do sums, write, etc., according to the rules. So on the one hand there are rules for behavior and on the other, there is communicating knowledge. I think we can offer this clarity without rewarding or punishing. Children will more readily tend to live according to behavioral rules if they were involved in their making. Give them insight into the effect of their behavior and leave them the freedom to develop their own morality (Köhler). Limit the number of rules. Every time we make a rule, we can think: is this rule really necessary? Can we think of another way of meeting our needs? Can we replace the rule with a request?

Support in acquiring knowledge in any field either at school or at home (for instance learning to clear up, wash up, take care of the environment) can be offered by stimulating the child's ability to discover things for himself (by imitation, asking questions, listening to stories, looking things up in books or on the internet, watching TV) and by giving feedback. Feedback can be given by saying what agrees with the knowledge gained in the past or with certain agreements and what doesn't. Giving marks or compliments can in my estimation eventually become redundant.

- *Making suggestions.* If we present our ideas about how we would like children to behave in the form of suggestions, there is no reason to punish them if they don't do as we tell them or to reward them if they do. They were, after all, only suggestions.

- *Establishing boundaries.* Children need boundaries, because knowing where they lie gives a sense of calm and safety. We might consider a boundary as a stone against which a child will bump, chafe and scrape while forming its character and view of the world. I propose no longer to guard these boundaries with rewards and punishments, but by standing up for our own values and those of the family or school, society and nature. Emphasize them again when a child oversteps these values in your eyes. If a child continues to overstep a boundary, it is important to direct our attention to his motivation. By nature, children tend to want to please. Their contrariness, whether expressed in nonchalance or in violence, means that something is troubling them.

- *Address needs.* Whatever a child says or does, he does it to fulfill a particular need. A punishment or reward is the result of our judgment and ignores what the child really needs. Look for the underlying need. If a child is using tragic means to fulfill his needs help him to find strategies beneficial to both himself and to others.

- *Set an example of social behavior.* Children seek ways to make themselves and others happy. People are social animals and generally prefer to live with other people. We can make it easier for children to find their own way in this by setting them an example with our own social behavior. This also applies to taking care of ourselves as described in Chapter 10. We can't make children into what we would like them to be. We can only give an example and wait to see what they do with it. They will accept from us only what suits their own personalities.

- *Create space for children's inner motivation.* I enjoy being in the background myself and watching children play, learn and live by their own inner motivation. As soon as I pounce on them and do my best to inculcate them with what I see fit, all I see and hear is myself.

For centuries, parents and teachers alike have tried to raise children like good little soldiers, marching to orders. There have always been people who realized that it is important to see and respect the child's own self. I hope that, after reading this book, more people will be more sparing in their use of punishments and rewards, so every child's self can come into its own.

Your children are not your children.
They are the sons and daughters of Life's longing for itself.
They come through you, but not from you,
And though they are with you, yet they belong not to you.

You may give them your love, but not your thoughts,
You may house their bodies, but not their souls,
For their souls dwell in the house of tomorrow, which you cannot visit, not even in your dreams.
You may strive to be like them, but do not seek to make them like you.

Kahlil Gibran, early twentieth century

LITERATURE

d'Ansembourg, Thomas (2007). *Being Genuine*. California, Puddle Dancer Press.

Gibran, Kahlil. *The Prophet*. Republished by different companies, a.o. UK, Penguin.

Hart, Sura and Kindle Hodson, Victoria (2006). *Respectful Parents, Respectful Kids*. California, Puddle Dancer Press.

Kashtan, Inbal (2003). *Parenting from Your Heart*. California, Puddle Dancer Press.

Köhler, Henning. *Difficult Children. There is no such thing*. London, Rudolf Steiner Press.

Kohn, Alfie (1999). *Punished by Rewards*. Boston, Houghton Mifflin.

Krishnamurti. *Krishnamurti on Education*. New Delhi, Orient Longman Ltd.

Martin, William (1999). *The Parent's Tao Te Ching*. New York, Marlowe & Company.

Mol, Justine (2007). *De Giraf en de Jakhals in Ons*. (not published in English yet)

Rosenberg, Marshall B. (2003). *Nonviolent Communication. A Language of the Heart*. California, Puddle Dancer Press.

Rosenberg, Marshall B. (2003). *Life-Enriching Education*. California, Puddle Dancer Press.

Solter, Aletha (1998). *Tears and Tantrums. What to do when babies and children cry*. California, Shining Star Press.

ABOUT THE AUTHOR

Justine Mol (1949) was born in a Dutch Catholic family. She was the seventh child of ten. She raised three children of her own and has supported her present partner in guiding his two teenage-daughters towards becoming who they are. You could say she is an experienced mother.

In 1999 she read an article on Nonviolent Communication by Marshall Rosenberg and in September 2004 she was certified as an international NVC trainer. In the course of these years she started writing articles on NVC and the Raising of Children. She also translated two books into Dutch: *The Inside Story, Understanding the Power of Feelings*, and *Teaching Children to Love* by Doc Lew Childre, both books published by the Institute of Heart Math in California.

After *Growing up in Trust* she wrote *De Giraf en de Jakhals in Ons (2007) (The Giraffe and the Jackal in Us)*. Besides writing she gives trainings and lectures on her books and on NVC in the Netherlands and abroad, and guides people through personal processes in individual coaching.

B O O K S

O is a symbol of the world, of oneness and unity. In different cultures it also means the "eye," symbolizing knowledge and insight. We aim to publish books that are accessible, constructive and that challenge accepted opinion, both that of academia and the "moral majority."

Our books are available in all good English language bookstores worldwide. If you don't see the book on the shelves ask the bookstore to order it for you, quoting the ISBN number and title. Alternatively you can order online (all major online retail sites carry our titles) or contact the distributor in the relevant country, listed on the copyright page.

See our website www.o-books.net for a full list of over 500 titles, growing by 100 a year.

And tune in to myspiritradio.com for our book review radio show, hosted by June-Elleni Laine, where you can listen to the authors discussing their books.

mySpiRitRaðio

SOME RECENT O BOOKS

9 Days to Heaven
How to make everlasting meaning of your life
Teresa O'Driscoll

This book offers a tactile and tangible way to feel closer to God's world. The meditations are truly moving and inspiring. I highly recommend 9 Days to Heaven to anyone seeking to invite conscious contact with God at any level.
Reneé Killian-Dawson, author

1905047738 128pp £9.99 $17.95

Christianity in 10 Minutes
Brian Mountford

If you want to begin at the beginning with the Christian faith, I can't think of a better way than by sitting down and reading this little book through. Plain-spoken, straightforward, succinct, here is a fresh intro-duction to the essentials-what Christians believe, how and why they believe what they do, what difference it can all make. If you've been around churches all your life and never fully grasped what it's all about, this is a superb refresher. If Christian faith is brand new to you, what a helpful first step you're holding in your hands.
Rev. Dr. Sam Lloyd, Dean of the National Cathedral, Washington DC

1905047096 64pp £4.99 $8.95

Contemporary Creed
A mini-course in Christianity for today
John Morris

This is a great "little book" for study and personal devotions, reading during Advent and Lent, and as preparation for Holy Baptism and/or Confirmation.
Episcopal Life

Powerful, remarkable and thought-provoking. Don't miss it!
UKCBD

1905047371 176pp **£5.99 $14.95**

God at Eventide
A devotional diary
A. J. Russell

35th printing
This powerful sequel to God Calling has a message of hope and comfort forged out of adversity. It has touched the hearts of millions.

1903019419 260pp 135/95mm **£5.99** cl.
US rights sold

God in the Bath
Relaxing in the everywhere presence of God
Stephen Mitchell

This little book is destined to become a spiritual classic. The many spiritual pearls of wisdom found in this book connect the Christian journey of faith with the odyssey of life. A wonderfully refreshing and invigorating reading of Christianity.
Nigel Leaves, author of *Odyssey*

1905047657 112pp **£9.99 $19.95**

God's Space in You
Melvyn Matthews

2nd printing
A simply written but accessible book that will give inspiration and help to those wishing to pray from within, in the business of this world.

1842981013 96pp b/w illustrations 135/05mm **£4.99**
US rights sold

Keylines
Ann Henning Jocelyn

Anne Joycelin has been developing a following throughout the country and, indeed, Europe, for her poetic reflections on love and loss, growth and relationships. A book of hope and comfort for all points of life's journey.

1846940435 160pp **£9.99 $19.95**

Other Temptations of Jesus
Lenten studies for adventurous Christians
John Henson

The Christian life is not about giving up, but taking up. The call of Jesus to discipleship is a positive one-love God and your neighbour. It's not about being serious, but happy and loving. Lenten studies for adventurous Christians. Recommended by the **Archbishop of Canterbury, Rowan Williams.**

1842981404 128pp **£7.99**

Other Communions of Jesus
Eating and drinking the good news way
John Henson

In these studies Christians are challenged to return to the mind of Jesus by allowing all the evidence of the gospels to be put into the balance. We have reversed his intentions. Communion should be a means of inclusion, not exclusion. Although the author's prime purpose is devotional, there are revolutionary implications. Should the churches take the contents of this book seriously, communion will never be the same again.

1905047495 220pp **£11.99 $24.95**

Perfect Freedom
Why liberal Christianity might be the faith you're looking for
Brian Mountford

2nd printing
Wonderful, lively and robust explanation and defence of a more liberal attitude to Christianity. If you want to know what liberal

Christianity is like in a few punchy sentences and a good deal of honesty from the author then this book is for you.
The Door

1905047185 108pp **£9.99 $15.95**

The Prophet of the New Millennium
Principles for an unprincipled age
Greg Dark

The Prophet of the New Millennium is not an alternative to Gibran's book, it is a complement to it. Today's world is very different to Gibran's. The political atlas has had to be modified frequently. This provides the ethical equivalent. It does not seek to define principles, or to provide answers, but it does seek to help readers find their own questions.

1905047576 128pp **£9.99 $16.95** cl.

Psalm
The world's finest soul poetry, told in a contemporary idiom
Peter Owen-Jones

Psalms are song lyrics, the poetry of the soul. Written around 2500-3500 years ago, they are part of our history, our consciousness. This selection, taking its inspiration from rap and country and western, brings the intent of the writers into the poetry and language of today.

1903816912 32pp 135/90mm **£4.99 $8.95**

True Stories

These inspiring true-life stories of faith, heroism and endurance, of suffering and humiliation, repentance and glory, trace the impact of the Christian faith down the ages and into the present day, into our own lives.

About the Bible 1905047347
About the Passion 1905047363
Of Conversion 1905047355
All illustrated, 128pp, **£5.99 $9.95**

The Wandering Sage
Timeless wisdom from our alternative teachers
Robert Van de Weyer

This collection of over 70 stories of Mulla Nasrudin captures the flavour of timeless wisdom and counter-cultural wit that is part of our Heritage. The stories are suitable for all ages, easy to remember, and once remembered never forgotten.

1903816653 128pp 205/130mm **£4.99 $7.95**

Created in the Image of God
A foundational course in the Kabbalah
Esther Ben-Toviya

This book provides a foundational course in the Kabbalah which speaks to the universal truths of the human experience, and is relevant to people of all backgrounds. It is a life changing, interactive course using the ancient tenets of the Kabbalah to pass on to you the experience of your unique place in the Eternal Worlds and to open your pathways of conscious conversation with the Higher Dimensions for everyday living.

1846940079 272pp **£11.99 $21.95**

The Wise Fool's Guide to Leadership
Short spiritual stories for organisational and personal transformation
Peter Hawkins

This is a real gem of a book. Many readers will be familiar with the Sufi tales involving the holy fool Mulla Nasrudin. Here Peter Hawkins applies the Nasrudin treatment to management consultancy and the results are hilarious. Essential reading for anyone working in an organisation.
Scientific and Medical Network Review

1903816963 160pp **£7.99 $11.95**

Son of Karbala
The spiritual journey of an Iraqi Muslim
Shaykh Haeri

A new dawn has appeared in spiritual travelogue with the publication of Son of Karbala. It deserves a place among the great spiritual odysseys of our time, right next to Gurdjieff's Meetings with Remarkable Men, which it at once resembles and exceeds in its honesty and clarity.
Professor Bruce B. Lawrence, Duke University, Durham NC

1905047517 240pp **£14.99 $29.95**

The Thoughtful Guide to Islam
Shaykh Haeri

About as timely as any book can be, should be read, and re-read, not only by so-called Christians but by many Muslims too.
The Guardian

Thoughtful without being an academic textbook, Shaykh Haeri shows us the completeness of Islam and gives many insights. The scope of this Thoughtful Guide is impressive.
Sangha

1903816629 176pp **£7.99 $12.95**

The Thoughtful Guide to Sufism
Shaykh Haeri

A Sufi is a whole human being, primarily concerned with the "heart" that reflects the truth that exists within it beyojnd time and in time. The aim is to reach the pinnacle of "his" self by achieving physical silence. The Sufi path is one of self denial. I found this book an absorbing and heartfelt source of information.
Sangha

1903816637 128pp **£9.99 $14.95**

You Called My Name
The hidden treasures of your Hebrew heritage
Esther Ben-Toviya

We are entering a new era of Jewish-Christian dialogue. This offers the reader a guided tour of Judaism, the religion of Jesus, that will enhance

the spiritual lives of all who follow the religion about Jesus, Christianity. This is more than a book. It is a cherished resource.
Rabbi Rami Shapiro, author of *The Divine Feminine.*

1905047797 272pp **£11.99 $19.95**

1000 World Prayers
Marcus Braybrooke

This book is the most comprehensive selection of prayers from different traditions currently available. It is divided into five major sections: God (including silence, love, forgiveness), times and seasons, the changing scenes of life, the world and society, and the natural world. There is a contemporary as well as traditional flavour.
Scientific and Medical Network Review

1903816173 360pp 230/153mm **£12.99 $19.95**

Meditation: the 13 Pathways to Happiness
Jim Ryan

This book shows you how to meditate step by step, in an easy-to-follow and friendly guide. Each chapter is clarified and embellished by a meditation that enables the reader to reflect on and experience what has been said. Stories and quotes bring home it's relevance for millions of people from ancient times to the present.Used as a course by thousands around the world, these words are now published for the first time.

190504772X 80pp **£9.99 $19.95**